D0991514

DALE EARNHARDT

The Pass in the Grass

and Other Incredible Moments from
Racing's Greatest Legend

The Charlotte Observer

Sports Publishing, L.L.C.
www.SportsPublishingLLC.com

DALE EARNHARDT

The Pass in the Grass
and Other Incredible Moments from
Racing's Greatest Legend

Supervising Editor: **Joseph J. Bannon Jr.**
Art Director: **K. Jeffrey Higgerson**
Director of Production: **Susan M. Moyer**

Imaging: **Christina Cary** and **Kenneth J. O'Brien**
Research Assistants: **Joanna L. Wright,**
Lynnette A. Bogard, and **Howard D. Fair**
Photo Researcher: **Davie Hinshaw,** The Charlotte Observer
Proofreader: **David Hamburg**

©2001 The Charlotte Observer
All Rights Reserved. No part of this book may be reproduced in any form or by any electronic or mechanical means including information storage and retrieval systems—except in the case of brief quotations embodied in critical articles or reviews—without permission in writing from its publisher, Sports Publishing, L.L.C.
Audio Credits, Photo Credits, and Copyrights at Back

ISBN 1-58261-439-3

The Charlotte Observer

Sports Publishing, L.L.C.
www.SportsPublishingLLC.com

Audio Table of Contents

Table of Contents

"Dale can be as good as anybody I ever worked with."
—Crew Chief J.C. "Jake" Elder

The future starts now

by Tom Higgins

BRISTOL, Tenn.—Dale Earnhardt, a rookie for whom stardom had been predicted several years down stock car racing's rocky road, showed Sunday that the future is now, whizzing to victory ahead of veterans Bobby Allison and Darrell Waltrip in the Southeastern 500 at Bristol International Raceway.

Earnhardt, 27, son of the late, legendary short-track star Ralph Earnhardt of Kannapolis, pulled away from his more experienced rivals in a 23-lap dash to the checkered flag, much to the delight of a crowd estimated at 26,000.

"I know that somewhere there's a fellow that's got a big smile and is mighty, mighty proud and even more happy than I am, if that's possible," said Earnhardt, referring to his father, who died of a heart attack in 1973.

His eyes moistened a bit, as did those of crew chief J.C. "Jake" Elder.

Ralph Earnhardt

"It's by far the biggest win of my career, no question," Elder said with much emotion, belying his reputation as a tough ol' "kingmaker" who has built winners for such superstar drivers as Fred Lorenzen, David Pearson, Benny Parsons and Waltrip.

"Dale can be as good as anybody I ever worked with," he said firmly.

Earnhardt, making only his 16th start on the NASCAR Grand National tour, averaged 91.033 mph in earning $19,800 from the record purse of $110,650.

Waltrip was leading when the final, sixth caution flag was waved.

"I knew with so little distance left to go that the key was getting out of the pits first," said Elder. "I'd told the crew we just had to do it. . . ."

The crew did, and Earnhardt rewarded their effort, getting a good jump when flagman Chip Warren unfurled the green and never losing any of that advantage.

When Warren exchanged the green for the checkered, the Osterlund crew embraced and danced jigs while members of other teams came over to offer congratulations.

"I know that somewhere there's a fellow that's got a big smile and is mighty, mighty proud and even more happy than I am, if that's possible."

Earnhardt, the Kannapolis youngster born and bred to racing, went around in unusually slow fashion, savoring the moment and the fact that all those predictions made in his behalf had been realized.

Only difference is, his future is now.

"The next thing I remember was flying (to the hospital) in a helicopter."

Earnhardt's wreck 'a fuzzy dream'

by Bob Myers

CHARLOTTE, N.C.—Dale Earnhardt is something of a dream walker, and darn glad that he can walk and dream.

Earnhardt doesn't remember much about the awful crash of his race car at Pocono, Pa., two weeks ago Sunday. To him, he says, it's like a fuzzy dream.

The physical pain—from two broken collarbones, concussion and severe bruises of the neck and chest—is subsiding. But the uncertainty of whether he'll be out of action for four to six weeks or longer and unable to defend his

current points lead toward rookie of the year honors gnaws at his innards.

Earnhardt, wearing a shoulder harness and still weak from his ordeal, wants to drive in the Aug. 25 race at Bristol, Tenn. He won his first Grand National Winston Cup race there in April. No rookie had won on the circuit in five years.

But a reporter suggested, "That's a tough place on collarbones. You're running over 100 mph on a half-mile track and turning every seven seconds."

"Naw, it wouldn't be that hard," he said Friday, brushing aside any suggestion of potential problems. "I'm the best on short tracks.

"I vaguely remember going down the backstretch and the tire letting go. The next thing I remember was flying (to the hospital) in a helicopter.

"The doctor in charge told me that judging from the way the collarbones were broken, it was an act of God my neck wasn't broken, too," Earnhardt said.

"I might have a bruised heart, but it's not broken."

Bobby Allison and Dale Earnhardt

If there is anything Earnhardt has learned from having to face this adversity, it's the concern shown by others.

"I thank God that I have more friends than I ever imagined," he said. "I cannot believe all the calls, messages and remembrances I've received.

"I might have a bruised heart, but it's not broken."

"Rod Osterlund and I have agreed on a five-year deal with three option years . . . and I couldn't be more tickled."

Osterlund issues Earnhardt a five-year ticket to ride

by Tom Higgins

CHARLOTTE, N.C.—Dale Earnhardt is one young auto racing driver who won't have to worry about where his next "ride" is coming from.

Earnhardt, a 28-year-old Kannapolis native, acknowledged Thursday he has signed a long-term contract with Osterlund Racing, the Derita-based team whose cars Earnhardt drove to NASCAR's 1979 rookie-of-the-year championship on the Winston Cup circuit.

"Rod Osterlund and I have agreed on a five-year deal with three option years . . . and I couldn't be more tickled," Earnhardt said from his Lake Norman home. "Talk about job security, I've got it. It frees me to concentrate on winning races and going for the driving championship, and believe me, that's a tremendous plus."

"Rod's as tickled as I am, 'cause now he won't have to listen to rumors all the time about his driver quitting and going to another team.

"We spent last year learning each other and we're ready to go now," continued Earnhardt. "I expect us to make a vast improvement over '79 because now we know how to work with each other."

"*The two years I've been on the Winston Cup circuit many of the veterans have good-naturedly always called me 'Boy.' Now several of 'em, including Junior Johnson, have offered congratulations and called me 'Champ.'*"

Lucky in Vegas

by Tom Higgins

LAS VEGAS, Nev.—Dale Earnhardt's good fortune didn't change when he flew to Las Vegas Saturday night for 18 hours of fun after winning the Winston Cup stock car driving championship via a fifth-place finish in the L.A. Times 500.

First, Earnhardt walked into the room reserved for him by sometime-race driver Mel Larson, whose full-time job is public relations director at the Circus-Circus Hotel and Casino. Dale's eyes bulged, as did those of his younger brothers, Randy and Donny, whom he had brought along from hometown Kannapolis.

They were in an elaborate suite with ceiling-high mirrors, gaudy chandeliers, a fully stocked bar, a spiral staircase, a piano and three bedrooms. One bed, elevated and surrounded by wall and ceiling mirrors, must have been 20

feet across.

"Gol-l-l-l-e-e-e!" said 29-year-old Earnhardt, mimicking television character Gomer Pyle. "This is as big as most houses back home."

Then Earnhardt, driver for the Rod Osterlund-Wrangler Team, took to the gaming tables. Within a half-hour or so, Earnhardt won $500 playing blackjack—as if he needed it.

With fifth place at the Ontario (Calif.) track, he pushed his season winnings to $464,860, excluding $50,000 for victory in last February's Busch Clash for 1979 pole winners.

The Winston Cup championship is estimated to be worth another $300,000 in bonuses, personal appearance fees and endorsements.

And it almost didn't happen.

Earnhardt and his crew made two big errors that could have meant losing the championship.

First, there was miscalculation when to pit during the first yellow flag period. That put Earnhardt a lap down, once as far as 11 positions back of point challenger Cale Yarborough of Sardis, S.C. If the race had finished that way, Yarborough and his team would have taken the title easily.

Then, after Earnhardt regained that lap, there was a communication breakdown on what was to be a final gasoline-only pit stop. Three lug nuts were taken off the right rear wheel for a tire change when Earnhardt was told to go and sped off.

"It's embarrassing, but what can you say? It happened," said Earnhardt.

"It's a wonder the wheel didn't come off and put me in the wall. . . . We were lucky, but that's part of it."

The Earnhardt-Yarborough showdown—heightened by their Chevrolets starting 1-2—didn't materialize in the early stages. Only once did they vie for the lead, on Lap three, when Earnhardt challenged but was held off.

"It's a wonder the wheel didn't come off and put me in the wall. . . . We were lucky, but that's part of it."

After that, Earnhardt retreated, and by Lap 60 was nearly lapped by Darrell Waltrip and Richard Petty, whose Chevys—destined to be sidelined with blown engines—appeared to be the fastest cars. On Lap 69 the yellow flew, seemingly saving Earnhardt, but the hasty pit stop cost a lap anyway.

Then the Earnhardt-Yarborough duel materialized. From Lap 156 to 176 of the 200-lap chase, they maneuvered for the lead in a two-car draft before a crowd generously estimated near 40,000.

Shortly after, Earnhardt and crew made their second mistake, and Yarborough began having tire problems. He finished third—behind winner Benny Parsons and Neil Bonnett.

That outcome enabled Earnhardt to become the only second-year driver to be the champ.

There's another important factor that "means about as much to me as anything," Earnhardt said.

"The two years I've been on the Winston Cup circuit, many of the veterans have good-naturedly always called me 'Boy.' Now several of 'em, including Junior Johnson, have offered congratulations and called me 'Champ.' "

"I just never thought that I would get a driver of Dale Earnhardt's capabilities and a sponsor like Wrangler."
—Richard Childress

Childress gets his wheels of fortune

by Tom Higgins

CHARLOTTE, N.C.—Through the years, auto racing insiders generally have agreed that all veteran driver Richard Childress, who fields his own cars, needed to win was adequate financial backing.

Childress, a Winston-Salem NASCAR competitor, is going to get it.

Only thing is, he'll just be preparing the cars and serving as team owner and manager. He'll leave the driving to Dale Earnhardt.

Dale Earnhardt and Richard Childress

It was strongly rumored that Earnhardt, considered one of the most promising young drivers, would wind up in the Junior Johnson organization along with another relatively young star, Darrell Waltrip.

The Observer learned Tuesday night that defending Winston Cup champion Earnhardt, who quit J.D. Stacy's team Sunday and took his big-buck Wrangler Jeans sponsorship with him, has decided to join longtime friend Childress.

The new teammates' first race will be the Champion Spark Plug 400 at Michigan International Speedway on Aug. 16. Doug Richert, 20, the crew chief who helped Earnhardt win the Grand National title last year in his second season on the circuit, will be a crew member.

It was strongly rumored that Earnhardt, considered one of the most promising young drivers, would wind up in the Junior Johnson organization along with another relatively young star, Darrell Waltrip.

Childress was the choice, as he agreed to end his 12-year driving career that has produced no victories, but almost $800,000 in winnings in 284 starts.

"*Dale has this urge to run over everything in his way to get to the front.*"
—Team Owner Bud Moore

Rollin' in the Rebel

by Tom Higgins

DARLINGTON, S.C.—Dale Earnhardt, a challenger but never a champion in five previous Winston Cup stock car races this season, wasn't to be denied Sunday in a thrilling CRC Rebel 500.

Driving his Ford on the ragged edge of control at Darlington Raceway, Earnhardt held off Cale Yarborough's passing attempt by half a car length at the finish line.

It was Earnhardt's first triumph since the National 500 at Charlotte Motor Speedway in October 1980, the year he won the NASCAR driving championship. That's a stretch of 39 races.

Cale Yarborough

It was the first victory at the 1.366-mile track for Bud Moore of Spartanburg, Earnhardt's car owner and crew chief, since he fielded a winner for Darel Dierlinger in the 1966 Southern 500, 31 events ago at Darlington.

"I knew we had Cale beat when I glanced to the left and didn't see anything at the flagstand," said a beaming Earnhardt, 30. "I figured he was going to swing toward the apron, so when I came off the fourth turn going to the checkered flag I started fading."

Fading?

"Yeah. Pulling to the inside where he was going."

"I knew it was very close, but I also knew I got beat," said Yarborough.

Bill Elliott drove his Ford to third place, and Benny Parsons took fourth in a Pontiac. Both finished in the lead lap. Tim Richmond finished fifth in a Buick, a lap down.

Earnhardt had led every race this season. In two of them he earned a bonus for leading the most laps in the race. But mechanical troubles or wrecks not of his making prevented him from winning. His best 1982 showing had been a second in the Valleydale 500 at Bristol, Tenn., the only event in which he was still running at the finish.

"We knew we could win if the car would just stay together."

The list of potential challengers steadily dwindled from the start. Pole-winner Buddy Baker went out after two laps when the flywheel on his car broke. . . . Harry Gant smacked the fourth turn wall. . . . Neil Bonnett crashed between Turns 3 and 4. . . . Richard Petty and Morgan Shepherd blew engines.

"We knew we could win if the car would just stay together," said Earnhardt.

"Why, I was so close to Neil and Slick (Johnson) in those crashes that I needed a can of Right Guard!"

"If I'm going to win another Grand National championship this year, or anytime soon, I had better get back in a Chevy to do it."

Smiling in a photo finish

by Tom Higgins

TALLADEGA, Ala.—Dale Earnhardt swept to the most satisfying victory of his career Sunday, taking a Talladega 500 thriller that could rank as motorsports' greatest race.

Earnhardt, fuming all week because he felt his driving style had been impugned, whipped into the lead in Turn 3 during a last-lap charge at Alabama Motor Speedway. He held on to first place when a pack of rivals went abreast in his wake and began dicing for position down the homestretch of the 2.66-mile track.

There were 10 drivers in the lead aerodynamic draft, and any of them conceivably could have won.

Terry Labonte, leading at the start of the final lap before a crowd of 94,000 and a national CBS-TV audience, appeared to salvage second place in a photo finish with Buddy Baker, Bobby Allison and Cale Yarborough.

However, two hours after the race, second was awarded to Baker with Labonte third.

Finishing fifth through 10th were Darrell Waltrip, Harry Gant, Lake Speed, Tommy Ellis and Bill Elliott. A NASCAR-record 15 drivers completed all 500 miles.

There were 68 lead changes among 16 drivers, both event records.

Baker led 41 laps, one more than Earnhardt. Yarborough, the pole winner at a record 202.474 mph, was in front 34 laps, Labonte 19 and Allison 16. Other leaders were Ron Bouchard, Trevor Boys, Elliott, Geoff Bodine, Dave Marcis, Gant, Ellis, Neil Bonnett, Ken Ragan, Clark Dwyer and Waltrip.

Earnhardt's 1.66-second margin of victory was the biggest advantage any driver held under the green flag.

"Just call me 'Stroker,'" Earnhardt, 33, said with an impish smile when he arrived in the press box for the winner's interview.

Early in the week some drivers were quoted as saying Earnhardt had become a "stroker" or gone conservative. That was cited as the reason for his leading the point standings toward the Grand National championship, which he won in 1980.

It had Earnhardt seething.

"Just because I hadn't won this year, they were taking shots at me," said Earnhardt. "I'd finished second four times, right on the bumper of the winners almost, and I was supposed to be stroking. Now that doesn't make sense."

The outcome padded Earnhardt's lead in the point standings to 65 over Labonte.

Earnhardt, who won $47,100 Sunday for the Richard Childress-Wrangler team of Winston-Salem, became the first driver to win back-to-back Talladega 500s. He averaged 155.485 mph in the 10th triumph of his career, as seven yellows slowed the pace for 38 laps.

Two of the cautions were caused by scary Elliott Forbes-Robinson and Trevor Boys wrecks, but neither was seriously hurt.

"This undoubtedly is the most exciting race I've ever been involved with," said Earnhardt, the 12th different winner this season, tying a modern-era NASCAR record established last year. "There always seemed to be 10 or 12 of us up there fighting for the lead. Every little bit, you'd find yourself racing someone else for position."

Earnhardt, driving a Chevrolet, took an unusual outside route to make the decisive pass of Labonte's Chevy.

"Terry favored the inside route the last few laps," said Earnhardt. "So the last time around I just held mine straight and went outside, because I figured it was too muddy to race in the infield."

Earnhardt grinned.

"My crew chief, Kirk Shelmerdine, was yelling over the radio as I came through Turn 4: 'Drive that thing! Drive it!'" said Earnhardt. "I started to answer him with something cute, but about that time I saw Buddy and Terry side-by-side in my mirror, and I pretty well knew it was mine. So I just waved at the crew and the fans down the homestretch toward the checkered flag."

"You waved and it was that close?" someone asked incredulously.

"Yeah, I was a-waving," came the reply. "I was tickled to death. Still am."

Earnhardt said Baker's following along as he (Earnhardt) began the move on Labonte was a critical factor. "Fortunately Buddy sensed what I was going to do and came out with me," he said. "It's not that he was trying to help me or Terry, he was trying to win the race himself. But it happened that his draft gave me a boost."

Earnhardt said Labonte slowed the pace the last few laps, "but I wasn't about to go around and give him the slingshot position." Because of the aerodynamics, second place generally is favored on the last lap at this speedway.

"It was tough here, like always, and we had a lot of pressure because of a big gamble right at the end."

Surviving bumper cars

by Tom Higgins

MARTINSVILLE, Va.—Dale Earnhardt scored a "smashing" victory Sunday in a rough, wreck-strewn Goody's 500, in which one grinding accident helped runner-up Darrell Waltrip move to within 23 points of NASCAR Grand National standings leader Bill Elliott.

The suddenly luckless Elliott was the major victim of a multicar crash on the 343rd of 500 laps at Martinsville Speedway. He wound up 17th—33 laps behind Earnhardt and Waltrip.

As a result, Elliott, who won his 10th race of the season just three weeks ago, lost much of his points lead for the third straight race. He dropped 63 points Sunday after leading by 206 Sept. 1.

Earnhardt collected $37,725 for his fourth stock car racing victory this season, all of which have come on the so-called short tracks.

"I earned every penny of it today," said a beaming Earnhardt, 34, after edging Waltrip in a duel of Chevrolet drivers. "It was tough here, like always, and we had a lot of pressure because of a big gamble right at the end."

That came with only eight laps to go on the .526-mile track when Bobby Hillin spun in Turn 3, bringing out the last of 12 yellow flags.

Earnhardt, Darrell Waltrip and Harry Gant were running 1-2-3 at the time.

"Finally, I said, 'Let's gamble,'

and I didn't come in."

Waltrip and Gant whipped into the pits for two fresh tires each, while Earnhardt stayed on the track.

"I was asking the boys in my pits (the Richard Childress team) by radio what they wanted to do," Earnhardt said. "They were asking back what I wanted to do. Finally, I said, 'Let's gamble,' and I didn't come in."

The field went back to full speed on Lap 497, all except Gant, who'd taken on a flat tire.

While Gant pitted, Waltrip maneuvered alongside Earnhardt on the backstretch. With a race record crowd of 37,000 cheering, Earnhardt cut the third corner close, forcing Waltrip to back off slightly, and he was unable to get in passing position.

"*Even Dale Earnhardt laughed about it, and he had just had his heart carved out by a gas gauge.*"

Funny? It's a gas.

by Ron Green

DAYTONA BEACH, Fla.—If it hadn't been dripping with irony, it would have been funny.

Aw, to heck with irony. It was funny.

Even Dale Earnhardt laughed about it, and he had just had his heart carved out by a gas gauge.

The Daytona 500 had ended Sunday, and the cars were circling the track one more time after the checkered flag had waved over Geoff Bodine. And there was Bill Elliott's Ford, battered in a midrace multi-car wreck and slapped around again in a supermarket parking lot fender bender on pit road. And it was pushing Dale Earnhardt's stalled Chevrolet back to the pits, the lame helping the lame. Along the way, they stopped and picked up Ron Bouchard's dead mount as well.

"Bill was the cleanup man, I reckon," said Earnhardt. Even he thought it was funny, and he had just seen a dreamy chance at winning the sport's richest race disappear with three laps to go when he ran out of gas.

Elliott had led qualifying and won a 125-mile race. Earnhardt had won the Busch Clash, which matches pole winners from the previous year, the other 125-mile race and a 300-mile sportsman race.

Sunday's 500-miler was supposed to be their show with Bodine's Chevy lurking in the wings.

Elliott, who had a charmed, 11-win, $2 million season in 1985, finished two laps down in 13th place. His agony was prolonged. Earnhardt's came like a sucker punch.

With three laps to go, Bodine was running in front and Earnhardt was an inch or two behind, exactly where he wanted to be. He would wait until the last lap, then use the peculiar aerodynamics of these high-speed tracks to slingshot around. It was all but inevitable. Being second on the last lap here is better than being first. Bodine slowed, hoping Earnhardt would go around, but he knew better. "I think if I had gone down pit road, he would've followed me," said Bodine.

Elliott and Earnhardt had been the names on the marquee over the past several days, between them winning everything there was to win in the elaborate preliminaries.

But halfway through the 197th turn around the 2-mile course, Earnhardt looked at his gas gauge and said, "Aw, no," or something like that. The needle normally stays around 6 or 7. When it drops to 5, you're running on fumes. His read 3. He had no choice but to drive onto pit road as Bodine sped away.

Earnhardt's engine died in the pits, and a crewman shot ether into it to get it restarted. When Earnhardt hurried back out to try for the highest finish he could manage, the ether detonated, broke the engine and left him sitting on the backstretch, nothing more than a spectator while cars flew by. By the time the thing ended, he had been dropped all the way back to 14th.

But as he climbed out of his car in the garage, he smiled and said, "Well, bleep.

"If I hadn't run out of gas, it would've been a helluva finish, wouldn't it?" said Earnhardt. "Who knows what would've happened?

"But when you see the gas gauge go down, what can you do? You come in and get some gas."

Earnhardt seemed remarkably placid after his 15th-round knockout when he was in position to become the only man to win four races at Daytona during a single Speed Week session. He didn't throw any tool boxes or kick his car or eat a wrench.

"I can take losing just like I can take winning," he said. "Ain't nothing to complain about. It's been a helluva week for me.

"But now the party's over."

"Richard was our key to winning the championship. His effort as team owner put us where we are. All the glory is his."

Earnhardt wins points title

by Tom Higgins

HAMPTON, Ga.—Whoever said you can't have it all forgot to tell Dale Earnhardt. Charging characteristically, Earnhardt swept to a record-smashing Atlanta Journal 500 victory Sunday, and in the process clinched NASCAR's rich Winston Cup Series stock car racing championship with one race remaining.

The triumph, combined with Darrell Waltrip's 39th-place finish after leaving the Atlanta International Raceway event with a failed engine on the 85th of 328 laps, left Earnhardt, 35, who also won the championship in 1980, with a 278-point lead going into the season finale Western 500 at Riverside (Calif.) Raceway on Nov. 16. The most points Waltrip could gain even if Earnhardt finished last in that race is 148.

It marks the first time since Cale Yarborough clinched with two races remaining in 1978 that the chase for the championship hasn't extended to the final race.

"Dale Earnhardt and Bill Elliott might just as well have been a couple of ol' redneck boys at Charlotte Motor Speedway on Sunday, juiced up with a bellyfull of bourbon, whopping each other up against the fence and raisin' hell."

Pass the dirt and some moonshine, boys

by Ron Green

CHARLOTTE, N.C.—For three years now, NASCAR has been trying to find a suitable home for The Winston, a race featuring its brightest stars.

May we recommend holding it next year at a rural dirt track? Way, way out in the country, where people still carry sidearms and make moonshine. On a Saturday night.

Dress the drivers in flowered print shirts, blue jeans, white socks, street shoes and some of those funny-looking old helmets.

Dale Earnhardt and Bill Elliott might just as well have been a couple of ol' redneck boys at Charlotte Motor Speedway on Sunday, juiced up with a bellyfull of bourbon, whopping each other up against the fence and raisin' hell.

But this was grim business they were about Sunday. When drivers start turning left or right into each other with malice aforethought at speeds of more than 150 mph, it is deadly grim. There's enough risk in stock car racing without having

someone try to take you out with a 3,500-pound weapon moving at high speed.

We chuckle at some of the little incidents that crop up fairly regularly in auto racing. Rubbing fenders, as they call it, blocking somebody, bumping someone from the rear to tell him to get out of the way, that sort of thing.

But Sunday's performance was terrifying. And, at whatever expense, including suspension, it ought to be the last we see of that kind of tactic.

Earnhardt tells it one way, Elliott another. Other drivers have their own versions.

Early in the last segment of this three-chapter race with a $150,000 difference between first money and second, Elliott hit Geoff Bodine, spinning him between the first and second turns.

Elliott says Earnhardt hit his right rear panel, causing him to lose control and run into Bodine. Tim Richmond, following close behind, verified that version. Earnhardt contended he didn't touch either.

"We'll have to see what NASCAR has to say about that. It was a little bit unsportsmanlike, I thought."

On the next lap, Elliott forced Earnhardt off the track into the infield grass on the front straight. Two laps later, Elliott had a tire go down, almost wrecking him. He said it was the result of Earnhardt's hitting him, forcing his fender in and cutting the tire.

"When a man pulls over and lets you beside him, then tries to run you into the wall, is that racin'?" Elliott said.

But he slammed into Earnhardt on the backstretch after Earnhardt had won the first prize and was taking a victory lap.

"That bothered me," Earnhardt said. "We'll have to see what NASCAR has to say about that. It was a little bit unsportsmanlike, I thought."

Unsportsmanlike! Those two had been playing a deadly game of bumper car and Earnhardt's talking about sportsmanship? Gimme a break.

Two drivers who had choice seats for much of this war were Bodine and Richmond.

Bodine, who has been a vocal critic of Earnhardt's style in the past, said, "You race hard and you do everything you can, you even rub and bang with people, but you don't try to kill them.

"If he thinks that's racing, he's sick. I don't care if it was for $200,000 or $2 million, and I'd tell him this to his face, my life is worth more than $200,000."

Richmond said, "It was worth being in third (where he finished) just to watch the show. It was like bumper cars that last 10 laps.

"I watched that fiasco. I guess no matter how many boos there are (Earnhardt heard plenty before and after the race), you've gotta keep doing your deal. I think if I got all those boos, I'd have to rethink.

"It's not his fault. They're letting him get away with it."

All in all, an ugly and shameful day for Winston Cup racing.

Besides that, except for the last 10 laps, the race was lousy.

"It was worth being in third just to watch the show. It was like bumper cars that last 10 laps."

—Tim Richmond

"We had a tire go right in front of the chicken-bone grandstands on the backstretch."

Drumstick ruins drum roll

by Ron Green

DAYTONA BEACH, Fla.—What Rusty Wallace and Darrell Waltrip and Terry Labonte and others couldn't accomplish with their snapping, growling 3,500-pound racers in the Daytona 500 Sunday, a chicken bone may have.

Beg pardon? A chicken bone?

That was the sniffy suggestion tossed out by Dale Earnhardt after he cut a tire less than a mile from the finish when it appeared he would win a race he had dominated like Secretariat.

That allowed Derrike Cope, who had lurked near the front all day, to go by him for the victory and three others to pass him as well.

The only grandstands at Daytona International Speedway other than those on the front straight is a small section of bleachers at the end of the backstretch. The cheap seats.

It was there that Earnhardt ran over something that cut his tire.

"We had a tire go right in front of the chicken-bone grandstands on the backstretch," said ol' Ironhead, making no bones about it. "I hit some debris, something. I heard it hit the bottom of the car and then it hit the tire and then the tire went.

"If I had known that debris was back there, well, there ain't nothing you can do. You can't see everything on the race track."

Especially a chicken bone.

"Richard [Petty], in my opinion, is in a class by himself, both on and off the track. To have people mention my name in the same breath with that man is about as big an honor as I could ever hope for."

From dirt tracks to the Grand Ballroom

by Tom Higgins

NEW YORK, N. Y.—Dale Earnhardt's earliest memory of stock car racing traces through time to the late 1950s.

Then, as a five- or six-year-old, he stood on the seat of a passenger car or pickup truck at the side of his legendary father, the late Ralph Earnhardt of Kannapolis, as Dad towed souped-up coupes to dirt short tracks around the Carolinas for weekend shows, most of which he won.

Dale Earnhardt's latest memory of stock car racing is of standing on the stage Friday night in the elegant Grand Ballroom of the Waldorf-Astoria, warm applause washing over him as he was honored for winning the NASCAR Winston Cup Series championship a fourth time.

The 1990 title gives Earnhardt four, second only to Richard Petty's seven, and the $1.3 million in bonuses accompanying it push his career winnings to $12,827,634, tops for all forms of motorsports.

Bud Moore, for whom Earnhardt once drove, "just simply the best overall that's ever been."

Not many can be found to dispute the grizzled Moore's contention, especially after Earnhardt's nine-victory 1990 season that produced world-record single-year winnings of $3,089,056.

Never mind that his 48 career triumphs tie him for only ninth place all time, well below the 200 wins of Petty.

"Richard is the King, and always will be," said Richard Childress, a former driver himself who gave up the wheel in 1981 when he was able to hire Earnhardt to drive his Chevrolets. "But I have to agree with Bud. Dale is achieving all these things at a time when there are 20 to 25 competitive teams capable of winning rather than just five or six."

Earnhardt is modest in his thoughts on that matter, and on the fame and wealth and international adulation of motorsports fans that he commands.

"Being the champion a fourth time is a little overwhelming," he said. "It took some time to sink in that I'd broken out of a tie at three titles with drivers as great as Lee Petty (Richard's father), Darrell Waltrip, Cale Yarborough and David Pearson. And that it left me three behind the King with, I hope, a lot of racing years left.

What a journey three decades-plus have produced for the tow-headed lad with the mischievous twinkle in his eye from those days he spent idolizing his dad.

"I think I watched every foot of every lap he ever run after I started going to races with him and Mom," Earnhardt, 39, said Saturday at the Waldrof, where he and his family spent the week as series sponsor R.J. Reynolds Tobacco Company's guest in the $4,000-per-night Presidential Suite.

"And I was almost always at his elbow there in the garage in the backyard of our house on Sedan Street in Kannapolis, trying to see what he did that made his cars so strong."

Dale decided to become a race driver, too, in the early 1970s, wheeling his own "little ol' 1956 Ford six-cylinder" at Charlotte's Metrolina Fairgrounds Speedway.

Devastated when his father died of a heart attack in the mid-1970s, Dale almost quit. But the sensation of speed generated by unmuffled engines had become too much a part of him. He stuck with it to become, in the opinion of NASCAR pioneer team owner

"Richard, in my opinion, is in a class by himself, both on and off the track. To have people mention my name in the same breath with that man is about as big an honor as I could ever hope for.

"Richard Childress and the crew guys likely aren't going to get as much credit for this season and what we've done together in the past seven years.

"I'm not just saying this now, but this championship means more than the others, even that first one in '80, although it came in just my second year in the Winston Cup. I was younger then, and a heck of a lot wilder, and I didn't appreciate everything that winning meant. I do now.

"A big reason it stands out is that we had to race so hard to get it. Mark Martin and that team of his that Jack Roush owns gave us more than we wanted to have to handle.

"Friday night was the warmest in New York for me for a lot of other reasons, one of them being that it was the first time my mama, Martha, got to come to the Waldorf and be at the awards program in person. Her being here means a lot to me. I just wish Daddy could have been, too, 'cause he never has left my heart."

It's likely Ralph Earnhardt, inducted into the National Motorsports Press Association Hall of Fame in 1989, was there. Invisible, certainly, but there at Dale's shoulder just as Dale had stood at his on the front seat en route to a race more than 30 years ago.

"*I'm not just saying this now, but this championship means more than the others, even that first one in '80. . . . I was younger then, and a heck of a lot wilder, and I didn't appreciate everything that winning meant. I do now.*"

"The best car doesn't always win.
We proved that last year."

Daytona 500: This can't be happening...

by Tom Higgins

DAYTONA BEACH, Fla.—Ernie Irvan, his Chevrolet almost out of fuel and sputtering, although running slow under caution conditions Sunday, won a Daytona 500 that turned from boring to bizarre as three accidents altered the outcome in the last 40 miles.

"I ran out of gas under the last yellow flag with still about a lap to go," Irvan said after the stunning finish in the NASCAR Winston Cup Series opener at Daytona International Speedway.

"I said, 'This can't be true. This can't happen to me.'"

It didn't, although runner-up Sterling Marlin, alongside Irvan in a Ford, thought it might.

"Ernie's car was sputtering so bad when we got to Turns 3 and 4 I thought it was going to stop," Marlin said. "I was saying, 'Quit! Quit! Quit!' But it didn't."

The race's twists and turns also undoubtedly left Dale Earnhardt, Darrell Waltrip, Davey Allison, Rusty Wallace and Kyle Petty uttering, "This can't be happening."

"The best car doesn't always win. We proved that last year," said Earnhardt, who finished fifth.

After a yellow flag, Earnhardt led the restart on Lap 194, but on Lap 198, Earnhardt's car lost its aerodynamics and spun out of control off Turn 2, wrecking both the Ford of Allison and Kyle Petty's Pontiac.

This created another caution period and with just two laps left Irvan was home free—if he had enough gas.

He did.

Barely.

"From early in Dale's career I've said if there ever was a natural-born race driver, he is it."

—Ned Jarrett

The best ever?

by Tom Higgins

HAMPTON, Ga.—All that Dale Earnhardt has to do Sunday to win the NASCAR Winston Cup Series championship is lift a finger.

With that, Earnhardt will flip the ignition switch of Richard Childress racing's Chevrolet to start the Hardee's 500 at Atlanta Motor Speedway.

When Earnhardt takes the green flag for the last of the season's 29 races, the title and approximately $1.3 million in bonuses are his, no matter what happens afterward.

It is to be a fifth championship for Earnhardt, 40, second only to Richard Petty's seven.

Earnhardt's success in big-time stock car racing's modern era, which began in 1972, has stirred considerable speculation among those who follow the sport closely:

Is he the best driver ever?

The main argument of those who feel Earnhardt is the most talented is this:

Although Earnhardt has "only" 52 victories, four this year, to the record 200 lifetime of Petty, Earnhardt's wins and titles have come during a more competitive period.

It's pointed out that when Petty, 54, was winning so big in the 1960s the schedule included up to 60 races. The fields weren't always filled in those days at some short tracks, and often only two or three other cars anywhere near the equal of Petty's were present.

Starting in '72 the schedule has ranged from 28 to 31 races, and since Earnhardt took his first title in '80, at least a dozen first-class cars ran every event.

Earnhardt, who leads Davey Allison by 156 points and Ricky Rudd by 165, seems embarrassed by the suggestion he's the all-time best.

"There is only one Richard Petty, and he's the King," Earnhardt has said repeatedly. "I don't think there's a comparison. . . . I could never top him as far as being a better driver.

"I've never thought about being the best or greatest. Not even when I started out in what amounted to jalopies back in the mid-'70s. I just wanted to drive a race car like my daddy."

"If I can keep going strong as Harry Gant is, then the chance should be there. Harry is 11 years older than me and he's won five races this year. . . . If I can stay in as good a shape as Harry has, and I plan to, I should have 10 more pretty good seasons of racing left."

Dale's father was Ralph Earnhardt, a two-time NASCAR national champion in the sportsman division, now known as the Grand National Series. The elder Earnhardt, rated by some as the greatest dirt track driver ever, died in 1973 of a heart attack.

Earnhardt concedes he hopes to equal or even surpass Petty's record for championships.

"If I can keep going strong as Harry Gant is, then the chance should be there," Earnhardt said. "Harry is 11 years older than me and he's won five races this year. . . . If I can stay in as good a shape as Harry has, and I plan to, I should have 10 more pretty good seasons of racing left."

Earnhardt already holds the motorsports record for prize winnings. His Winston Cup total is $13,909,874. Darrell Waltrip is second with $11,024,517.

Where do the experts rate Earnhardt in terms of all-time ability?

Very highly, but short of having him dethrone Petty.

Said Ned Jarrett, a two-time Winston Cup champion and now a broadcaster:

"From early in Dale's career I've said if there ever was a natural-born race driver, he is it. He just seems to have an uncanny ability to do incredible things with an automobile. He can save them when they're so far out of shape it's amazing."

"It's good to get back in Victory Lane."

Pit, and make it quick

by Tom Higgins

CHARLOTTE, N.C.—Dale Earnhardt, bedeviled by mostly bad luck at Charlotte Motor Speedway since 1986, battled back with the help of a brilliant green flag pit stop Sunday and held off Ernie Irvan to win a Coca-Cola 600 thriller.

No. 13 figured prominently as Earnhardt edged fellow Chevrolet driver Irvan by 39-hundredths of a second, or about three car lengths, before a track-record crowd estimated at 160,000.

The outcome:

- Ended Earnhardt's NASCAR Winston Cup Series non-winning streak dating to last September at 13.

- Snapped Ford's victory string dating to the same month at 13.

- Marked the second time in 65 races dating to 1960 at the 1.5-mile track that a Winston Cup event has been won from starting position No. 13, which is where Earnhardt lined up the Richard Childress team's Lumina.

Pivotal to all this was a sizzling 19.40-second pit stop by Earnhardt's crew, led by Kirk Shelmerdine, on the 346th of 400 laps.

It enabled Earnhardt to return to the track slightly ahead of Irvan and the dominant Pontiac of Kyle Petty, both of whom stopped 2 laps earlier for service that required 21.19 and 19.72 seconds, respectively. Earnhardt wasn't headed afterward, leading the final 54 laps—the only time he was in front in the race.

"It was a great pit stop. That was the key," said current Winston Cup champion Earnhardt after his 53rd career victory and fourth at his Charlotte home track, two in the 600. "Me being in front made Ernie and Kyle run a little harder and use their tires up.

"I got in quick, whoa'd down within the limits, got gone quick and flat-footed around through Turns 1 and 2 on the return lane. I fudged all I could on the speed limit (55 mph) on pit road without getting penalized. I judged 55 to be 4,000 rpms and I might have got up to about 4,050 leaving.

"For years Charlotte was a great place to me and then bad things began happening. It's good to get back in Victory Lane."

"I got in quick, whoa'd down within the limits, got gone quick and flat-footed around through Turns 1 and 2 on the return lane. I fudged all I could on the speed limit (55 mph) on pit road without getting penalized. I judged 55 to be 4,000 rpms and I might have got up to about 4,050 leaving."

"Earnhardt just sat in his driver's seat, staring straight ahead. He wiped his face, sipped some Gatorade and stared some more. A few minutes passed before he climbed out."

So much for Santa Claus

by Liz Clarke

DAYTONA BEACH, Fla.—With his mother praying in the infield and his father about to jump out of the CBS anchor booth, Dale Jarrett blew past a seemingly cursed Dale Earnhardt Sunday to win the Daytona 500 in the final two laps.

Earnhardt, gunning for his first win in 15 tries, led more than half the race in a powerful Chevy that had drivers scared all week.

But with three laps left, Earnhardt got wobbly and Jarrett took advantage.

He drove around rookie Jeff Gordon, who had been hugging Earnhardt's bumper for a good 20 laps, to pull even with Earnhardt with about a lap and a half left.

His power fading, all Earnhardt could do was bump him. Jarrett hung on, and with a push from Geoff Bodine's Ford, he found just enough to blow past for the win.

Earnhardt finished second.

He had won all three races leading up to Sunday's race, and was considered a favorite to win his first Daytona 500.

It seemed ordained early on. Earnhardt ran close to the front all day, and waltzed unscathed around the seven wrecks that took out strong cars like Kyle Petty's, Rusty Wallace's, Jimmy Hensley's, Ernie Irvan's and Al Unser Jr.'s.

Earnhardt took the lead for the last time on Lap 179. With the rest of the pack in single file behind him, it seemed a battle for second.

When Jarrett bolted, his father, Ned, a former driver who was analyzing the race for CBS, cheered him on from the anchor booth.

Dale Jarrett couldn't hear, of course, but obeyed instinctively.

"We've lost this race about every way you can lose it. We've been out-gassed, out-tired, out-run, out-everythinged."

> ## "I'm getting tired of winning everything up until the 500 and then not win it."

While Jarrett was being interviewed in the winner's circle, Gordon and Earnhardt pulled into the garage, one behind the other.

Gordon popped out at once and couldn't wait to talk about his fifth-place finish. "One heckuva day! One heckuva day! I couldn't ask for a better day!" Gordon said, beaming.

Earnhardt just sat in his driver's seat, staring straight ahead. He wiped his face, sipped some Gatorade and stared some more.

A few minutes passed before he climbed out.

"We've lost this race about every way you can lose it," Earnhardt said. "We've been out-gassed, out-tired, out-run, out-everythinged.

"It's tough to run the way we did all week, and have the success we've had all week and not win the big one. I'm getting tired of winning everything up until the 500 and then not win it."

"On the restart, he made some moves that chilled your blood and suddenly burst out ahead of everyone. Like magic."

Oh, so he's a magician...

by Ron Green

CHARLOTTE, N.C.—Had Houdini been there, among the multitude at Charlotte Motor Speedway Sunday night, he might've whistled and whooped and stomped his feet for Dale Earnhardt, and then sidled up beside him and said, "How'd you do that?"

As darkness settled over the countryside around the speedway, Earnhardt showed again why he's every race driver's worst nightmare.

Earnhardt, the wild one, the sliest of the sly and bravest of the brave, kept slipping out of deep trouble and somehow whipped that dreaded No. 3 through little cracks and crevices where angels fear to drive. And by the end of the Coca-Cola 600, he was out front and going away.

It must be magic.

Earnhardt doesn't just drive, he races. And shame on anybody who gets in his way.

Earnhardt was twice penalized, once for breaking the rules, once for being a bad boy. Total assessment was about a lap and a half, maybe 2 laps. Two to 3 miles.

Twice, he had to make up an entire circuit of the mile-and-a-half oval just to be up with the leaders, and twice he did it.

Earnhardt doesn't just drive, he races.

And shame on anybody who gets in his way.

Greg Sacks did. Earnhardt was in the process of trying to make up a mile or so that he had lost when he pitted under a green flag.

He was in a hurry and Sacks was in his way. Earnhardt drove up behind him and suddenly, Sacks was doing a samba, into the wall, across the track, onto the grass. This produced the caution flag Earnhardt needed to make up his lost ground but, whoa, NASCAR officials slapped a 1-lap penalty on him for rough driving.

"I was close, but I didn't hit him," said Earnhardt when it was all over. "Maybe our bumpers touched or I touched him a bit but it wasn't like I rammed the hell out of him. I don't think I nudged him." (And then, with a smile): "I might've been a-gin him."

When the green flag came out again on Lap 335, Earnhardt was a mile and a half behind and time was starting to become precious. So he did what he always does.

"I was runnin' the hell out of it," he said.

"I was close, but I didn't hit him," said Earnhardt when it was all over. "Maybe our bumpers touched or I touched him a bit but it wasn't like I rammed the hell out of him. I don't think I nudged him." (And then, with a smile): "I might've been a-gin him."

Hey, he's no angel.

When a caution flag allowed him to close big ground, you knew what was coming. On the restart, he made some moves that chilled your blood and suddenly burst out ahead of everyone. Like magic.

Earlier, he had been leading after 221 laps but had come in for gas and tires and had gotten a 15-second penalty for exceeding the 55-mph speed limit on pit road.

"Was I going too fast on pit road?" he asked the media after the race.

Who knew? Was he?

"I don't know but No. 28 (Davey Allison) was right behind me and he was gaining on me."

Oh, Earnhardt did hit Ernie Irvan. Ran into Irvan's rear end by accident, and admitted it.

Hey, he's no angel.

"It has been a bad year, losing both Davey and Alan. . . . I want them back. I'd gladly have run second to them today to have them back."

Davey Allison and Alan Kulwicki: A tribute

by Tom Higgins

POCONO, Pa.—Dale Earnhardt outran Rusty Wallace for a victory Sunday in a Miller Genuine Draft 500 thriller, but it was what the two did immediately after the NASCAR Winston Cup Series race that will likely be remembered most.

On the "cool down" lap after the checkered flag, Wallace thrust a flag bearing the No. 28 out the window of his Pontiac as he circled the 2.5-mile track. Earnhardt maneuvered his Chevrolet alongside Wallace, pointing to the flag to draw it to the attention of fans.

No. 28 is the numeral borne by the Ford Davey Allison drove so brilliantly for the Robert Yates Racing team of Charlotte. Allison, 32, died Tuesday of injuries he suffered Monday in the crash of a helicopter he was piloting.

Earnhardt then pulled to the start/finish line where his Richard Childress crew awaited with an even larger No. 28 flag.

As Earnhardt stayed in the car, the crewmen knelt around the machine in prayer. Fans seemed almost frozen in the grandstands.

Earnhardt then circled the triangular track clockwise, holding the flag.

It was a "Polish Victory Lap," a combination tribute to Allison and Alan Kulwicki, the 1992 Winston Cup champion who lost his life April 1 in the crash of a private plane.

As Earnhardt stayed in the car, the crewmen knelt around the

machine in prayer. Fans seemed almost frozen in the grandstands.

"It has been a bad year, losing both Davey and Alan," Earnhardt said after climbing from his car. "I want them back. I'd gladly have run second to them today to have them back."

Said Wallace: "We wanted to remember the Allison family today. I wish I could have done the reverse lap for Alan and brought the No. 28 flag out."

Earnhardt said, "I motioned for Rusty to go back around with me, but he didn't see me. I wish he had."

"I go back home to Kannapolis and Mooresville and I'm just one of the guys. It's impressive what someone from a small town can do and accomplish."

Dale takes the sixth

by Tom Higgins

HAMPTON, Ga.—It was a humble, close-to-tears Dale Earnhardt that emerged from Victory Lane late Sunday at Atlanta Motor Speedway to talk about his sixth NASCAR Winston Cup championship.

"It's really unbelievable to me," Earnhardt said. "I never even dreamed that I would someday be in Winston Cup racing. It's a miracle to me what we've accomplished. . . . I go back home to Kannapolis and Mooresville and I'm just one of the guys. It's impressive what someone from a small town can do and accomplish.

"I'm proud of that. I'm proud to be Ralph Earnhardt's son. And I'm proud of my team . . . bouncing back from a bad year like 1992, when we won only one race and finished 12th in the point standings."

Ralph Earnhardt, Dale's dad and a former NASCAR Sportsman Division champion, died in 1973 of a heart attack.

> *"I'm proud to be Ralph Earnhardt's son. And I'm proud of my team . . . bouncing back from a bad year like 1992, when we won only one race and finished 12th in the point standings."*

Earnhardt finished 10th Sunday and claimed the championship, worth a minimum $1.5 million, although Rusty Wallace won the race. Earnhardt finished 80 points ahead of Wallace, losing 46 points in the season finale.

"We wrapped the championship up before the race was over," said Earnhardt, who could have finished as low as 34th and still won. "We got it when at least eight cars were sidelined.

"Then, I went racing. I wanted to win the championship by taking the race. But I got a little too aggressive and too carried away with it and I got in trouble. Then I had to just ride.

"No matter whether you're a six-time champion or not, that don't make you King Kong going into the corner. It brought me back to earth."

Earnhardt, 42, was referring to a tangle with the Ford of Greg Sacks on Lap 225. The collision dented the side of Earnhardt's Chevrolet.

"No matter whether you're a six-time champion or not,

that don't make you King Kong going into the corner.

It brought me back to earth."

"And now, boys and girls, we can focus-s-s-s on winning the Daytona 500."

"In shooting for a seventh championship, which would tie Richard Petty's record, the pressure will be on from the press, our sponsor and ourselves. We've got the sixth one behind us now, and we can talk about shooting for it.

"And now, boys and girls," he said, grinning, "we can focus-s-s-s on winning the Daytona 500. Doesn't anybody want to ask when I'm going to win the Daytona 500? You want me to tell you about it now?"

Earnhardt hasn't ever won the sport's biggest race, which annually opens the season.

"I've got so many people to remember and thank it's unbelievable."

Seventh heaven in .06 seconds

by Tom Higgins

ROCKINGHAM, N.C.—Dale Earnhardt drove to a record-tying seventh NASCAR Winston Cup Series championship Sunday just as he'd hoped in the AC-Delco 500, charging hard for the race victory at N.C. Motor Speedway.

With the title that equaled the total of retired Richard Petty already assured when closest challenger Rusty Wallace fell out with engine trouble, Earnhardt outran Rick Mast to the checkered flag by less than a car length.

Earnhardt's Chevrolet flashed across the line .06 seconds ahead of Mast's Ford before a cheering crowd estimated at 55,000.

Members of the Richard Childress racing team, who have fielded the cars for six of Earnhardt's championships, streamed jubilantly onto pit road. Then, when Earnhardt took an extra victory lap, the crew led by Andy Petree stood atop the pit wall and bowed in salute.

Earnhardt dedicated the latest championship to the late Neil Bonnett, his best friend, who was killed Feb. 11 in a crash while practicing for the season-opening Daytona 500. He dedicated Sunday's win to the late Frank Wilson, the speedway president who died in August.

"I've got so many people to remember and thank it's unbelievable," said Earnhardt after his fourth victory this season, second at the track nicknamed "The Rock," and 63rd of his career.

Earnhardt had been reluctant to discuss the prospects of matching Petty's mark, once considered unapproachable.

Earnhardt, although holding a commanding 321-point lead over Wallace going into the 29th of the season's 31 races, had been reluctant to discuss the prospects of matching Petty's mark, once considered unapproachable.

"Now, we can talk about it all day long," said Earnhardt, who boosted his lead in the standings to an unbeatable 448 points over Wallace. The title is worth $1.25 million.

Earnhardt, who started 20th, led four times for 108 laps, including the final 77. He averaged 126.407 mph and earned $60,600.

"Working traffic and passing cars spectacularly, seven-time Winston Cup champion Earnhardt was third by Lap 195. On Lap 197 he ran down and passed Mark Martin for second place. . . ."

Maybe they should make it the Daytona 499

by Tom Higgins

DAYTONA BEACH, Fla.—Sterling Marlin withstood a stirring, dramatic charge by Dale Earnhardt during the Daytona 500's final 11 laps Sunday, and claimed the NASCAR Winston Cup season-opening classic for the second straight year.

The 500 is the only Winston Cup race Marlin has won. It's the only major event Earnhardt never has won in 17 years of trying.

Gambling on a pit stop for four tires during the crash-marred event's 10th and final caution period on Laps 187-189, Earnhardt was positioned 14th for the restart behind the other front-runners, who didn't pit.

Working traffic and passing cars spectacularly, seven-time Winston Cup champion Earnhardt was third by Lap 195. On Lap 197 he ran down and passed Mark Martin for second place.

It's the only major event Earnhardt never has won in 17 years of trying.

> *"This is the Daytona 500, and I don't reckon I'm supposed to win the . . . thing."*

Earnhardt ran down Marlin, too. But he couldn't pass him and finished runner-up for the third time. He also lists finishes of third, fourth and has been fifth four times in the 500.

"I saw Dale coming," Marlin said upon taking his Chevy to Victory Lane. "I was going to block him one way or another or I wasn't coming back the last lap. We'd have swapped some paint. Martin would probably have won the race."

"This is the Daytona 500, and I don't reckon I'm supposed to win the . . . thing," Earnhardt said. "If we'd had some drafting help we might have got by Sterling, but he was awful strong. I reckon the best car won. He deserved to win it."

No. 000001

"This Richard Childress racing team is hard to beat when we're right."

Big day at the Brickyard

by Tom Higgins

NDIANAPOLIS, Ind.—Dale Earnhardt held off Rusty Wallace and Dale Jarrett to win a Brickyard 400 thriller Saturday that appeared destined to be postponed by rain at Indianapolis Motor Speedway.

Thousands of the 300,000 fans who bought tickets had headed home and came rushing back to the grandstands when NASCAR officials finally got the Winston Cup cars on the historic 2.5-mile track four hours later than planned. The show was worth sprinting for, especially the final 25 laps following the event's only caution flag as Ford drivers Wallace and Jarrett tried to run down Earnhardt's Chevrolet.

Earnhardt flashed across the yard-wide strip of bricks forming the start/finish line .37 seconds ahead of runner-up Wallace and .904 seconds ahead of the third-place Jarrett.

"To win this race is great," said a breathless Earnhardt, who averaged 131.999 mph, a record for the two-year-old race. "This Richard Childress racing team is hard to beat when we're right.

"I've never won the Daytona 500, our biggest race. The Brickyard is next to it, and we'll sure take it.

"I heard a lot of talk this week that we're out of (the points race). I think winning at a place as big as Indy shows we aren't dead yet."

"I get along with Jeff, but we don't travel in the same circles. He plays video games, I go big-game hunting. He wears athletic shoes, I wear boots. What we have in common is that we love to race."

It's a win; It's a loss

by Tom Higgins

HAMPTON, Ga.—Dale Earnhardt scored a dominating victory Sunday in the NAPA 500 at Atlanta Motor Speedway, but it wasn't enough to overtake Jeff Gordon for the NASCAR Winston Cup championship.

Gordon clinched a first title for himself and Hendrick Motorsports when he led the 61st of the race's 328 laps for five bonus points. That gave Gordon, who started the season finale 147 points ahead of defending champion Earnhardt, the cushion he needed for the title worth a minimum $1.3 million.

After a strong early run, Gordon's Chevrolet developed handling problems and he finished 32nd, 14 laps down, winning the championship by 34 points.

"We didn't have a great day, but we had a great year," said Gordon.

"It's good to end a season so clean. But don't ask what it's like finishing second in points. Everybody knows what I think of second."

Earnhardt started his black Chevrolet in the 11th position on the 1.522-mile track. He swept into first place on Lap 18 and stayed ahead the rest of the way except during or shortly after pit stops.

"It's good to end a season so clean. But don't ask what it's like finishing second in points. Everybody knows what I think of second," Earnhardt said.

Earnhardt led six times for 268 laps, including the final 59, in averaging a track-record 163.632 mph, breaking his mark of 156.849 set in March of 1990. The victory was his seventh at the speedway, tying the retired Cale Yarborough for the most.

"This ended a good year for us," Earnhardt said after his fifth victory of 1995 and 68th of his career.

On Friday, Earnhardt, known for his all-out driving style, told reporters he was going to start "running on the careful side of the ragged edge."

However, on Lap 82 Earnhardt made a daring dive to the inside in Turn 3, and by the time he emerged from Turn 4, he had passed Gordon and Ford foes Ricky Rudd and Mark Martin in a stirring surge that had the crowd estimated at 135,000 screaming.

"I got up this morning feeling cocky," explained Earnhardt. "I love kicking fanny, and that's what the black car did today."

"Gordon is so young they're going to serve his team milk at the banquet . . . instead of champagne."

That's careful?

"I got up this morning feeling cocky," explained Earnhardt. "I love kicking fanny, and that's what the black car did today.

"I sort of filled you reporters full of bull Friday."

Earnhardt congratulated Gordon. However, Earnhardt, 44, couldn't resist teasing the youthful new champion.

"Gordon is so young they're going to serve his team milk at the banquet in New York instead of champagne," Earnhardt said of the series' Dec. 1 awards banquet.

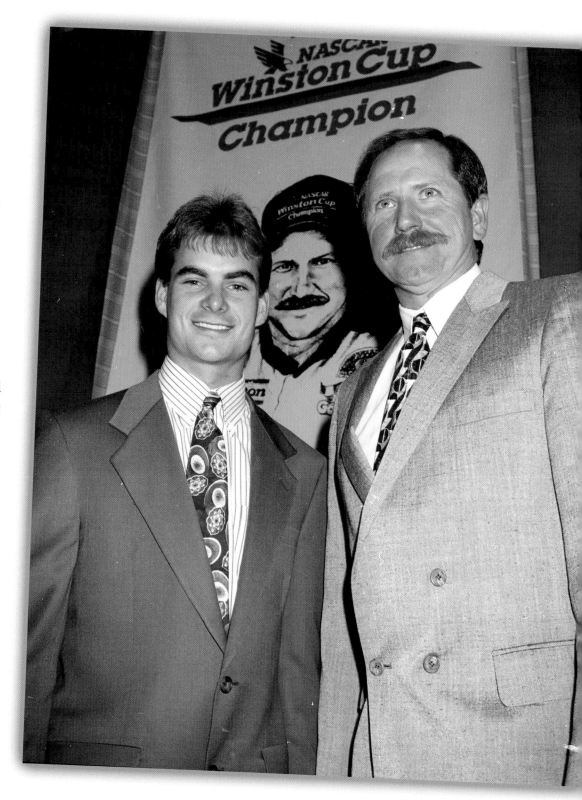

"When you move the guy in front of you out
of the way with a good whack at 100-plus
mph, you're going to enhance that
Intimidator image, no way around it."

A bumpy win, just like old times

by Ron Green

ROCKINGHAM, N.C.—Dale Earnhardt polished up his image as "the Intimidator" Sunday. Just when he was starting to look like a choirboy.

Even he has spoken, albeit briefly, about driving with a bit more caution now at age 44 than he did in his earlier days when he was earning his reputation as the nightmare in every racer's rear view mirror. But caution ran quivering for the exits Sunday when Earnhardt hooked up with Bobby Hamilton in a breathtaking, lead-swapping battle around North Carolina Motor Speedway.

With the Goodwrench 400 starting to wind down, Hamilton drove the red-and-blue No. 43 that Richard Petty made famous around Earnhardt's black racer into the lead. That lasted one lap. Earnhardt swept back around him.

So Hamilton swept back around Earnhardt. Then suddenly, Hamilton was sliding sideways, tagged by the Intimidator. Hamilton gathered his car up enough to keep it from wrecking, but it scraped the wall and when he opened his eyes, he was back in fifth place.

Earnhardt went on to win. It was his 69th Winston Cup victory. Hamilton, who has never won a Winston Cup race, spun out trying to make up his lost ground, hit the wall and finished 24th.

Earnhardt dismissed the incident as just a racing accident.

> "We were coming through the (fourth) corner and there are some bumps down there," he said. "We were bumping and we just bumped together."

Did you bump him or did he bump you?

> "I didn't turn the steering wheel to bump him. When we got together, I tried to get off him as fast as he tried to get off me," he said, his hawk-like features showing nothing in the way of emotion.

Hamilton saw it differently.

> "I haven't won seven championships (as Earnhardt has) and I haven't won 80-something races but I'm smart enough to know you don't do stuff like that this early in the season," he said. "That's an end-of-the-season move (when positions in the points race are at stake.) He plain hit me. It wasn't close at all."

A NASCAR spokesman testified in Earnhardt's behalf. He said, "We have a penalty box for certain situations. We use it when we're much more sure of an intentional move to advance a position or to create a caution period than we were today.

> "You saw a lot of hard racing all day. There was nothing we saw about that move to create a penalty box situation."

"We were coming through the (fourth) corner and there are some bumps down there. We were bumping and we just bumped together."

Earnhardt is an easy target in a situation such as this. His car is black, his racing uniform is black, therefore his heart must be black. He could have been as blameless as a baby Sunday but when you move the guy in front of you out of the way with a good whack at 100-plus mph, you're going to enhance that Intimidator image, no way around it.

It didn't help that the man he bumped was trying for his first Winston Cup victory and was driving a car owned by Petty, the King himself. And that Earnhardt was driving a Goodwrench-sponsored car in a Goodwrench-sponsored race.

Earnhardt looked down the road apiece, at what he called "the big picture," and said, "I'm just going to race whoever is there racing.

"We'll just see who's next to come up there and race, and see who wins."

He didn't mean it to sound like a threat but it did, like bring 'em on and I'll kick their tailpipes. When the Intimidator says it, it sounds, well, intimidating.

"You saw a lot of hard racing all day. There was nothing we saw about that move to create a penalty box situation." —NASCAR spokesman

"In a horrifying instant, Earnhardt's car was bumped by Sterling Marlin's and thrown into the air at more than 200 mph. When his car finally landed with its sheet metal twisted and torn, Earnhardt had a broken sternum and collarbone. He was fortunate to be alive."

The wreck, in detail

by Tom Higgins

TALLADEGA, Ala.—Dale Earnhardt realized he was facing a grim certainty Sunday when contact from a rival turned his leading Chevrolet sideways during the DieHard 500 at Talladega (Ala.) Superspeedway, NASCAR's fastest track.

"I knew I was going to hit the wall and I knew it was going to hurt," Earnhardt, in pain from fractures of the collarbone and sternum, said Wednesday at Indianapolis Motor Speedway.

Despite his injuries, Earnhardt is planning to drive in today's time trials for Saturday's Brickyard 400.

Although obviously in discomfort, Earnhardt managed to smile during a news conference in which he was joined by team owner Childress.

"I knew I was going to hit the wall and I knew it was going to hurt."

After expressing thanks to well-wishers, Earnhardt discussed the violent accident that produced his injuries.

"As we came through the tri-oval (homestretch) I looked in the mirror and saw the No. 4 car (Sterling Marlin) to my right rear and the No. 28 (Ernie Irvan) behind me," Earnhardt said. "Then, going toward Turn 1, I felt contact in the right rear and around I went.

"That's when I knew what was coming.

"I remember everything.

"When I turned abruptly into the wall is when I broke my sternum. Then the car got up on its side and slid along and I could see the asphalt pavement through the window net.

"I hunkered down as much as I could and I was gripping the steering wheel with both hands to keep from being thrown around in the cockpit, 'cause I knew following cars were going to hit me.

"I saw Derrike Cope coming and he hit me in the roof, mashing the front of the roof down toward the dash. Then Robert Pressley hit me, and I think this collision broke my left collarbone. As my car got back on its wheels, Kenny Schrader hit me."

Earnhardt grinned.

"Kenny told me, 'I seen you and I aimed for you,'" Earnhardt said.

"Smoke was rolling out from under the dash because a lot of wires were burning. I was hurting, but I was able to reach out and switch the battery off.

"I could hear Richard calling me on the radio. And I could hear Richard talking with my wife, Teresa, who had a radio. My radio wouldn't transmit, and I couldn't talk back.

"I remember the rescue crew getting to my car. Also a couple NASCAR guys. I told them not to cut the roof off, 'cause I thought I could get out with a little help.

"I did get out, and I wanted to lay down, but couldn't because of the pain. That's why I walked to the ambulance rather than getting on a stretcher."

"I did get out, and I wanted to lay down, but couldn't because of the pain. That's why I walked to the ambulance rather than getting on a stretcher."

"His ride around those last laps in that piece of junk might have looked funny to some. But to some, it looked noble."

Daytona just gets weirder

by Ron Green

DAYTONA BEACH, Fla.—At some point while he was wrecking, perhaps while he was upside down going about 190 mph, or maybe when he landed on top of Ernie Irvan's car, or when he was spinning wildly through traffic, Dale Earnhardt thought, well, so far, so good.

One moment, the man called the Intimidator had been in second place in the Daytona 500 as the last laps of a wild and wonderful race wound down. The next moment, he was sideways and airborne and upside down and against the wall and spinning and generally in a fix.

"I didn't hear no loud bangs and didn't feel any hard crashes so I figured I must be OK so far."

The thousands watching from the grandstands held their breaths. This could be bad. Just Thursday, he had said, "I feel like I'm bulletproof," but his black Chevy looked like it had been hit by cannon fire.

But then Earnhardt climbed out of the wreckage. "I didn't hear no loud bangs and didn't feel any hard crashes so I figured I must be OK so far," he said. "And then it stopped and I got out.

"I got in the ambulance and looked back over there and I said, 'Man, the wheels ain't knocked off that car yet.' I went back over there and looked at the wheels and I told the guy in the car (who was preparing to haul it away) to flip the switch, and it fired up.

"I said, 'Get out. I gotta go.'"

And he went. He climbed back into the remains of his car and drove it around the track to his pit. His crew went to work on it, ripping stuff off, taping stuff down, and Earnhardt took what was left back out to finish what he had started.

He's 45 years old, rich as an oil baron and has nothing left to prove to anybody, but as long as that ol' car would run, he was gonna drive it. Anybody else—anybody else—would have taken a seat in the ambulance and ridden off, and let the wreckers put that heap on a hook. But not ol' Ironhead.

It wasn't the triumphant ride for which he had hoped. He has won 70 Winston Cup races, has won 29 races of various types on this track and has been the Winston Cup champion seven times, and has won more than $28 million but he has never won the Daytona 500.

He thought Sunday might be the day. You could tell he liked his chances of finally ending the jinx. And there he was in second place with 11 laps to go, sitting there just waiting for the right time to make his move, and then suddenly the world was spinning every which way and pieces of his car were flying around like the sea gulls that hang around the speedway.

Jeff Gordon, who would go on to win the race, had started to pass him when the accident happened. The young champion said, "I saw his car push up (toward the wall) and give me an opening so I went. When he came back down off the wall, he hit me square in the door, which was lucky. If he'd hit me a little farther back, I would have been caught up in the wreck.

Earnhardt says he can get along fine without ever winning this race, but he can't. He's done everything else. He wants this one, because he's a racer.

"After the race (on the cool-down lap), I saw this mangled black No. 3 coming up behind me and I thought, 'Uh oh,' but he pulled up beside me and gave me a thumbs-up sign and I knew he understood I was just trying to do what he was trying to do, win the Daytona 500."

Earnhardt says he can get along fine without ever winning this race, but he can't. He's done everything else. He wants this one, because he's a racer.

His ride around those last laps in that piece of junk might have looked funny to some. But to some, it looked noble.

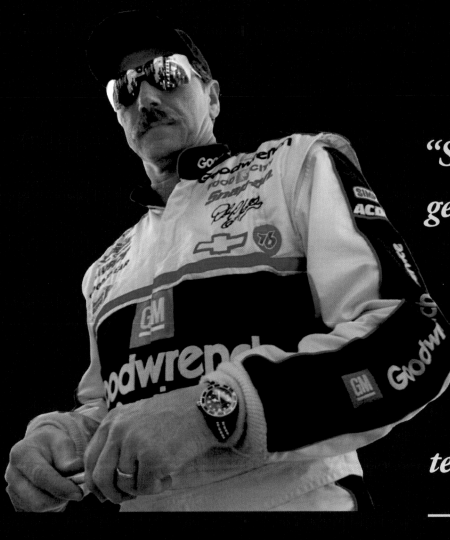

"Stress or heat, or getting too tired, might precipitate a little event where the brain short-circuits temporarily."
—Neurosurgeon
Dr. Charles Branch

Cleared to race

by David Poole

RICHMOND, Va.—Dale Earnhardt said Friday doctors did everything "other than taking me apart" in their search for the cause of last Sunday's blackout at Darlington.

"They dug and prodded and did everything they could do," Earnhardt said. "They worked awful hard on me and looked awful deep and found nothing, which is a great relief."

Dr. Charles Branch, a neurosurgeon at Bowman Gray Medical Center in Winston-Salem, said Earnhardt "had an episode that probably remains somewhat unexplained."

Branch said Earnhardt was cleared to race in tonight's Exide 400 at Richmond International Raceway after doctors reviewed an extensive battery of tests "to determine whether or not there was any medical condition that we could identify that . . . would put him at any further risk at continuing . . . as a race car driver, and we could find none."

Branch offered two possible explanations for the blackout, or what he called "a temporary dysfunction of the brain," which led to Earnhardt hitting the wall twice on the first lap and then missing pit road the first time he tried to find the entrance.

The first is that it was a migraine-like episode in which a blood vessel went into a spasm or contracted to restrict blood flow to Earnhardt's brain stem just long enough to create the dysfunction.

"This is not something you can treat or identify once it's gone," Branch said.

The second possible explanation Branch offered was a "short circuit" of the brain caused by an injury Earnhardt suffered years ago.

"Any contusion or bruise of the brain . . . can leave a little scar in the brain," Branch said. "Stress or heat, or getting too tired, might precipitate a little event where the brain short-circuits temporarily."

Branch said he could not tell Earnhardt the same thing won't happen again.

"The brain-wave testing and all the other testing we did were normal," the doctor said. "So whatever this was, was temporary and it's impossible to say if this will or won't happen again. But it doesn't appear likely."

The second possible explanation Branch offered was a "short circuit" of the brain caused by an injury Earnhardt suffered years ago.

"Daytona is ours! We won it, we won it, we won it!"

Beating the jinx

by Ron Green

DAYTONA BEACH, Fla.—The racing had gone from hard to fierce, the laps winding down under threatening skies, men with millions of dollars at stake driving 190 mph and taking chances that would scare the devil himself.

Dale Earnhardt was leading, as he had much of the afternoon, but you wondered what would happen this time to defeat him. This was the Daytona 500, and he doesn't win this race. He had won 70 NASCAR Winston Cup races and seven season championships and 30 other Daytona International Speedway races, but not the 500. Something always happened to keep him from winning his sport's biggest race. He cut a tire or ran out of gas or broke something or just got beat.

What would happen this time?

Everybody in the crowd of 180,000 was standing. On the next-to-last lap, there was a wreck on the backstretch, far behind the leaders, which meant the last lap would be run under caution and whoever crossed the finish line first on this 199th of 200 laps would win.

Cars gathered up in a growling cluster behind Earnhardt, banging into each other, clawing to get to the front. But they couldn't make it. Not this time.

The Great American Racer had won the Great American Race.

It may have been the most popular victory in the 50 years since NASCAR racing was born in this place, or certainly one rivaled only by Richard Petty's 200th win, in 1984.

It came out of the blue. Earnhardt, 46, hadn't won in his past 59 races. Questions arose. Would he ever win anything again, let alone the Daytona 500? Had he lost his daring, his reflexes, his desire?

He answered those questions Sunday, and the sport of racing smiled.

The Great American Racer had won the Great American Race.

As Earnhardt drove down pit road toward Victory Lane, hundreds of crewmen from other teams came out to congratulate him and to touch his hand as he drove by. Then, the man they call the Intimidator acted like a kid with a new toy. He drove into the infield grass and did a couple of doughnuts. And either because he's a heckuva driver or he was just lucky, when he had done his spins in the grass, the tracks were shaped like a 3, the number on his car.

Fans went out there and picked up some of the grass he had knocked loose and put it in their coolers, saving a piece of this moment. Some lay down in the tire tracks, to feel the place where Earnhardt had driven. And some stood in the tracks and had their pictures taken.

Mike Skinner, Earnhardt's teammate in the Richard Childress stable and one of his toughest competitors Sunday, yelled, "You're the man. You're a baaad man!"

In Victory Lane, Earnhardt said, "Daytona is ours! We won it, we won it, we won it!"

In the press box, he pulled a toy monkey out of his uniform shirt, threw it to the floor and shouted, "I'm here, I'm here, I'm here and I got that . . . monkey off my back!"

History would have been out of kilter if Earnhardt hadn't ever won the Daytona 500, the premier event in NASCAR Winston Cup racing. He has won everything else and in doing so has become the foremost figure in his sport. But this one was, of course, special, and as tough as he is, he had tears in his eyes on the last lap.

The past didn't haunt him on the closing laps.

"I wasn't thinking about what could happen," he said. "I was just doing what I had to do. I was working to keep my car in front until somebody turned me over or we got to the finish line."

During his post-race news conference, Earnhardt looked down to the infield and saw several dozen fans lined up to form a 3.

"Race fans are awesome," he said.

"Gosh, it was a great day."

"Race fans are awesome."

"You race for thousands of dollars. That's good. You race to win. That's good. Those are good reasons. But there's nothing wrong with wanting to make my dad happy."
—Dale Earnhardt Jr.

The son also rises

by Ron Green

MOORESVILLE, N.C.—It's lunchtime at Dale Earnhardt, Inc. and the man whose name is on the sprawling building is trying to eat spaghetti in his office while talking to a visitor.

A throbbing bass line from a car stereo thumps through Dale Earnhardt's office, providing an unwanted soundtrack to dinner hour.

Exasperated by the low-slung sound that beats, beats, beats its way inside the office walls, Earnhardt excuses himself, opens the front door and gives his 23-year-old son, Dale Jr., whose black Chevy Impala has become a rolling concert hall, a warning.

"Turn the music down or turn it off . . . now," Earnhardt barks at his son.

Kids.

Dale Earnhardt Jr. is still a kid in so many ways.

He lives rent-free in a double-wide trailer on property his father owns. He's got a set of drums he loves to bang on, he's always got a buddy or two hanging around his home, and if he's not driving his Grand National race car like he'll be doing Saturday in the Carquest Auto Parts 300 at Charlotte Motor Speedway, he's probably listening to music (he favors alternative bands) or playing on his computer.

"He still gets to be himself," says sister Kelley, who's three years older than Dale Jr.

But he's becoming a star.

In his first full season on the Grand National circuit, Dale Jr. has already won one race, finished second in two others and, keeping with Earnhardt tradition, flipped his car on the back straight at Daytona and then walked away from it.

He has already begun to live up to the enormous expectations that come with having a name framed by tire smoke and trophies.

He's so popular, industry insiders say sales of Dale Jr. merchandise already rank among the top 10 for all drivers—Winston Cup included.

"There ain't no pressure," Dale Jr. says, sitting below a framed photograph of his grandfather, Ralph, the inspiration of the Earnhardt racing family.

"I use it to my advantage. That's the only way this deal's going to work—if everything that could be a negative gets made into a positive."

It's not easy being the son of a legend.

In Dale Jr.'s case, it meant a childhood in which he rarely lacked for anything except the constant presence of his father. Dale Sr. has won seven Winston Cup points championships, 71 races and the hearts of thousands of fans.

He has already begun to live up to the enormous expectations that come with having a name framed by tire smoke and trophies.

But it came with a cost.

Dover. Daytona. Talladega. Bristol. Earnhardt was always somewhere else when Dale Jr. was growing up.

"There was an absence," Dale Jr. says. "We had good schooling and good opportunities because of him. But when you're a kid, you don't realize all of that.

"The family suffers but it's part of the job."

They had their moments together.

Like the summer afternoon when Earnhardt tried to teach his son to get up on water skis. To make it easier, Earnhardt put Dale Jr. on skis in shallow water behind a pickup truck, then drove him through the boat house.

"They drug me up on that concrete and skinned my rear all up," Dale Jr. says.

Then there was the time when Dale Jr. climbed into a go-kart for the first time. He hardly knew the brake from the accelerator and when he put his foot down, the go-kart climbed several feet up a guy wire holding a power line in place.

And there was always racing.

Earnhardt learned the sport by watching his father, a local hero. He hung around the garage, he tinkered with engines and he let racing become his oxygen.

Dale Jr. was the same way. He did odd jobs around the shop for his dad, gradually taking on more responsibility as he grew older.

"There was an absence. We had good schooling and good opportunities because of him. But when you're a kid, you don't realize all of that."

—Dale Earnhardt Jr.

After graduating from Mooresville High School in 1992, Dale Jr. attended a trade school for two years, then worked in his dad's Chevrolet dealership in Newton. He did oil changes, body work, whatever was necessary, learning his way into the business. Nothing was given to him.

He began racing street stock cars at Concord Motor Speedway when he was 17, building his own car while getting a hands-on feel for what his father did.

"If you pay attention, that's where you get good at what you do," Dale Jr. says.

Parked behind a maintenance building behind Earnhardt's race shop is the rusting shell of Dale Jr.'s first race car. Dead leaves litter the interior and the faded red paint is peeling off. It's an old Monte Carlo that Dale Jr. built, feeling his way into the sport.

"We've come a long way from that," Dale Jr. says, looking at his training wheels.

Now, in addition to being father and son, Dale and Dale Jr. are mentor and student, car owner (though stepmother Teresa Earnhardt officially owns Dale Jr.'s car) and driver.

It's difficult to separate the professional relationship from the paternal one.

When Earnhardt talks about Dale Jr.'s progress, you sense the pride. He keeps mentioning how well he's doing and how, at age 23, Dale Jr. is doing all the right things.

"I'm proud of him growing up the way he has. I feel he turned out pretty nice."

"He's an Earnhardt," the father says, referring to the aggressive driving style that has defined his career.

Earnhardt has guided Dale Jr. in racing without forcing his knowledge on his son. Earnhardt believes in his kids earning what they have.

"It's totally up to him," Earnhardt says. "Everything they (the kids) have done, apart from education, I've tried to let them decide about their life and how they live it."

Sometimes, Dale Jr. has strained at the leash. It led to a two-year stint at Oak Ridge Military Academy in Greensboro when Dale Jr. was in the seventh and eighth grades. Talking in class and running wild at times were all part of Dale Jr.'s personality for a time.

"I was always kept in a box, so to speak, under strict adult supervision," he says. "Anytime they opened it, I came out of that box."

Does Dale Jr. listen better now?

"Do they ever?'" his father says with a laugh.

"I'm proud of him growing up the way he has. I feel he turned out pretty nice."

Like most sons, Dale Jr. seeks his father's approval above all others.

"It's like a never-ending process earning his respect," Dale Jr. says. "It's bottomless. I get worn out by it at times. But it's something you always want. Sometimes it becomes more important than the job at hand."

It's Dale Jr.'s greatest incentive.

"What other reason do you race for?" Dale Jr. asks.

"You race for thousands of dollars. That's good. You race to win. That's good. Those are good reasons. But there's nothing wrong with wanting to make my dad happy."

When Dale Jr. won his first Grand National race at Texas last month, father and son flew home together.

Two months earlier, the Earnhardt family and close friends had gathered at 3 a.m. to welcome Dale Sr. home after his Daytona 500 victory.

In April, Dale Sr. called ahead to make sure family and friends did the same for his son.

"Dad brought him inside and told him congratulations," Kelley says.

It's after lunch now and Dale Jr. is on his way to being a star again.

He's got to hit the road for an autograph session in Salem, Va., and he's making sure he's got everything. Autograph cards he'll sign. Directions.

He's on his way.

"I'll see you later," Dale Jr. tells his dad as he turns to go.

"You be careful," Earnhardt, the father, says.

As the Impala pulls away, the music thumps to life.

"It's like a never-ending process earning his respect. It's bottomless. I get worn out by it at times. But it's something you always want. Sometimes it becomes more important than the job at hand." —Dale Earnhardt Jr.

"I'm sure he's going to have a lot of laughs watching me try to wheel that thing around there, and I'm sure my jaw will be on the floor watching him wheel his around."

—Dale Earnhardt Jr.

Dale Jr.'s debut ends with 16th-place finish

by Rick Bonnell

CHARLOTTE, N.C.—He's a drummer, a songwriter and occasional party animal. Someday soon, he'll be a pretty good racer, too.

The build-up far exceeded the performance, but Dale Earnhardt Jr. finished a respectable 16th Sunday at the Coca-Cola 600. It was Junior's Winston Cup debut and he finished 10 places behind his father-namesake.

Hype is like oxygen for stock-car racing, but anticipation of the 24-year-old's arrival on the top circuit was unprecedented. He started his workday with an ESPN live shot on Victory Lane—as close as he'll get to the place for a while. He was mobbed nearly everywhere he went, and sat in with the band on the drums during the Speed Street Festival Friday night.

"I don't remember anyone coming in who's gotten this much attention," said Ned Jarrett, who knows all about father-son racing legacies. "It's unusual to say the least. We might not ever see it again."

Junior thrived on it. Asked if he was relieved, he said, "I'm glad it went the way it did. I'd like every weekend to be like this."

Junior worked out of a generic white hauler for this race—sponsor Budweiser is still working on a paint job—but that was the only understated touch to his weekend.

"It was crazy. They were about to knock us down, smack (into) him. There were fans everywhere," said Gary Davis, one of the Budweiser officials guiding Junior through the crowd.

Dale Sr. decided the kid needed a laugh Sunday, so just before driver introductions, he asked his son if he wanted an autograph. Driver Ken Schrader's question was serious—he wanted an autograph from Junior, as a memento of the kid's big day.

After realizing Schrader wasn't joking, Junior signed the back of Schrader's race suit shortly before climbing into his Monte Carlo.

Things deteriorated quickly from there. After qualifying eighth in his first Winston Cup race, Junior dropped to 11th over the first lap and 15th over the second. By Lap 36, he fell out of the top 20.

He knew instantly his car didn't handle well, particularly when his father blew by him at the start.

"I don't remember anyone coming in who's gotten this much attention," said Ned Jarrett, who knows all about father-son racing legacies. "It's unusual to say the least. We might not ever see it again."

"It was terribly loose. I was just trying to stay out of everybody's way and not make a fool of myself."

—Dale Earnhardt Jr.

"It was terribly loose. I was just trying to stay out of everybody's way and not make a fool of myself," said Junior, the defending Busch Grand National champion.

He quickly learned the difference between Grand National—lighter cars and generally shorter races—and Winston Cup.

"The Busch guys run 300 miles. They drive flat-out all the time," Junior said. "I learned how these guys are patient. They don't race real hard until the end. They make sure they don't rip it up" early on.

The kid's a quick learner. Patient and steady through the second half of the race, he avoided any trouble. His first stop after the race was his father's hauler.

"I just wanted to make sure he was OK with how I ran as car-owner and father," Junior said.

"It was a decent night," Dale Sr. assessed. "We stayed out of trouble and Dale Jr. didn't collect me up there at the end."

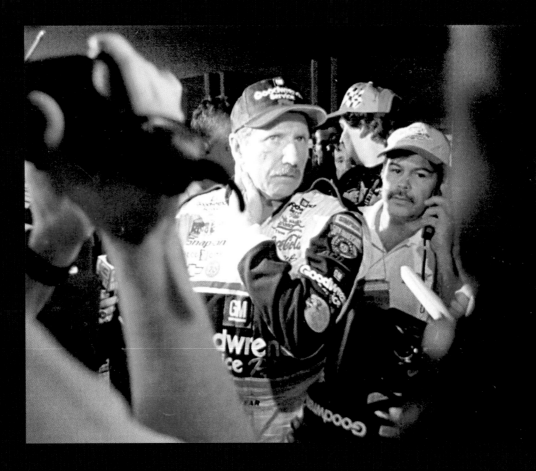

"That was one of the most unique, neat, exciting, fun—just everything you could describe and roll it all up into one—time I've ever had."

Door-to-door Dales in Earnhardt dream race

by David Poole

BROOKLYN, Mich.—Door-to-door Earnhardts, racing toward the checkered flag.

It happened Friday at Michigan Speedway, in the third leg of the 1999 International Race of Champions series, the showdown that Dale Earnhardt and Dale Earnhardt Jr., not to mention two generations of race fans, have hoped for.

They came off the final turn two abreast, son on the high side and father down low, banging sheet metal as they raced toward the finish. Earnhardt Jr. was ahead for a moment, but at the line it was Earnhardt the elder winning by seven-thousandths of a second—less than two feet.

"That was one of the most unique, neat, exciting, fun— just everything you could describe and roll it all up into one— time I've ever had," Earnhardt said after making it three-for-three in IROC races this year.

"I guess you couldn't write a better script," Earnhardt Jr. said. "I think that was the way it was supposed to be at this point in my career and this point in his career. It ended just the way it was supposed to end. I was trying with all of my might to win that race, but that's storybook right there."

Earnhardt started last in the 12-car field because he had won the two previous IROC legs at Daytona and Talladega. In each of those races, Earnhardt had led only the final lap. In both, he made his pass for the lead off the final turn.

So there was irony as well as drama in the air as Friday's race wound down. This time, Earnhardt had led since passing his son on Lap 27 in the 50-lap event. This time, Earnhardt would have to protect himself from a last-lap challenge he knew was coming.

"I knew he was going to run high and I knew he wanted to try that on the last lap," Earnhardt said. "I sort of figured out what his mindset was, and I was glad to see him be patient. That shows me that eventually he will win races in that situation."

"It ended just the way it was supposed to end. I was trying with all of my might to win that race, but that's storybook right there." —Dale Earnhardt Jr.

The emphasis there was on eventually, however, as Earnhardt wasn't about to roll over.

Earnhardt Jr. went high in Turn 3 in his orange IROC racer and pulled alongside his dad's blue car. Coming out of the fourth turn, Earnhardt Jr. nudged ahead, but he also sensed that he was in trouble.

"I knew the position I had wasn't going to win the race," he said. I knew 50 yards from the line, when I had him a foot or two, he would get back by me."

Earnhardt did. And no, at no point did he ever consider backing off to let his son get his first IROC victory.

"No way," Earnhardt said. "He's going to have to earn everything just like his dad did. I don't think he would have wanted me to let him win. He would have gone home and everybody would have said, 'Your dad let you win.' That wouldn't have been cool.

"Of course, they could say to me, 'Your son let you win it.' Bull. Look at the side of that race car."

Earnhardt's blue car had some serious scuff marks on the right side from their bumping battle off the final turn.

"He hit me pretty hard trying to stop my momentum," Earnhardt Jr. said. "I tried to hit him to stop his momentum. It was like 'You ain't going to win it! No, you ain't going to win it!'"

The back-and-forth continued as the son came to Victory Lane to join his father for an all-smiles, backslapping moment they both have dreamed of sharing.

"To come down and race side-by-side, door-to-door, and finish first and second was pretty awesome," Earnhardt said. "I don't know that we'll ever have that opportunity again, but we did and we experienced it. It's something we're going to cherish."

"He hit me pretty hard trying to stop my momentum. I tried to hit him to stop his momentum. It was like 'You ain't going to win it! No, you ain't going to win it!' "
—Dale Earnhardt Jr.

"I didn't mean to do it intentionally . . . but I know he's not going to see it that way."
—Dale Earnhardt

"Have you ever heard him say he means to spin anybody out?"
—Terry Labonte

Bristol dishes out more than some could take

by David Poole

BRISTOL, Tenn.—Cantankerous, aggressive and exciting.

Dale Earnhardt used those words to describe Bristol Motor Speedway Saturday night after his controversial victory in the Goody's 500.

The same words, of course, could also be used to describe the man who uttered them. He was certainly all three on a wild night that will keep Winston Cup race fans talking for weeks to come.

Terry Labonte had the lead with a half-lap to go until Earnhardt's Chevrolet hit Labonte's in the left rear and sent Labonte spinning on the backstretch. Earnhardt dove low around Labonte and beat Jimmy Spencer back to the checkered flag to win for the second time this season and the 73rd time in his Winston Cup career.

It was his first short-track win since a victory at Martinsville in 1995 and his first win at a non-restrictor-plate track since Atlanta in March of 1996.

> "Whether he checked up or I got in deeper or what, I bumped him too hard and turned him loose. It spun him."

"Terry caught me coming to the white flag in (turns) three and four and bumped me a little," Earnhardt said. "When we went back to Turn 1, I went back in there to get with him and get under him. Whether he checked up or I got in deeper or what, I bumped him too hard and turned him loose. It spun him.

"I didn't mean to do it intentionally. I meant to get in there and race with him, but I know he's not going to see it that way. I know he's upset. He has a right to be."

Labonte was doubly upset, actually. He took the lead from Earnhardt on Lap 439 and was on his way to victory until he slowed for a caution on Lap 491 and got hit from behind by Darrell Waltrip. That spun him in Turn 4, but he got new tires and the green flag with five laps to go. He sliced back toward the front and had grabbed the lead back as he and Earnhardt got the white flag. But he never made it back to the start-finish line and wound up eighth with a wrecked Chevrolet.

"Dale gave me a shot and turned me around," Labonte said. "That's the way it goes, I guess."

Earnhardt maintains that all he intended to do was to race with everything he had to take the victory away on the final lap.

"When you go into the corner after someone on the last lap and he checks up or you get into the corner harder or whatever, you've got no control of the speeds of the race car when you get together," he said. "I definitely didn't mean to go down there and turn him around. I was getting after it. I knew I was going to have to race him hard to get in the corner and try to get back under him."

"Dale gave me a shot and turned me around. That's the way it goes, I guess."

—Terry Labonte

Earnhardt maintains that all he intended to do was to race with everything he had to take the victory away on the final lap.

The controversy added another chapter to Bristol's history of eventful finishes. Labonte's last win in 1995, in fact, came when he took the checkered flag going sideways after a bump from Earnhardt in Turn 2. In the spring race in 1997, Jeff Gordon tapped Rusty Wallace loose in the final two turns and took away the victory.

The major development in the first half of the race was points leader Dale Jarrett's trouble. He spun on Lap 77 and then got hit from behind by Jerry Nadeau on Lap 99. The damage from those two wrecks put him behind the wall for more than 150 laps, and Jarrett wound up 38th. He lost 101 points from his lead over Mark Martin but still has a 213-point edge.

"We knew sooner or later it was going to happen," said Jarrett, who hadn't finished worse than 11th since the season-opening Daytona 500. "You can't ride without all the trouble all the time. We'll just take our lumps here and go on."

That's a sentiment several drivers might have shared after another typically wild evening at Bristol.

"I was just driving the car as hard as I could go and giving it everything I had. It was just that time of day. It wasn't time to take it easy."

Atlanta race answers the critics

by Jim Utter

HAMPTON, Ga.—Boring races? No problem.

Uncompetitive Chevrolets? No problem.

Illustrating the hard driving that earned him seven Winston Cup championships, Dale Earnhardt wiped away—at least for one weekend—the critics of his sport with a spectacular down-to-the-wire photo finish victory over Bobby Labonte in Sunday's Cracker Barrel 500 at Atlanta Motor Speedway.

In a race featuring 30 lead changes among 17 different drivers, Earnhardt took the lead on Lap 306 of the 325-lap race and held off repeated challenges by Labonte—

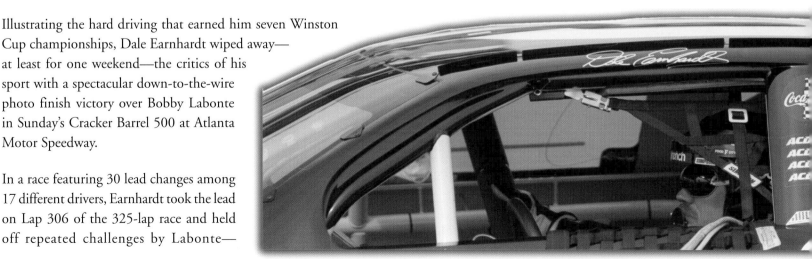

"It definitely wasn't a boring race."

including two attempts by the driver of the No. 18 Pontiac to pass him in the final 10 laps.

On the race's final lap, Labonte—who had won four of the past seven Atlanta races entering the weekend—came off Turn 4 alongside Earnhardt and they crossed the finish line side-by-side. But it was Earnhardt who was awarded the win by a scant 0.010 seconds—among the closest finishes in NASCAR history.

"It definitely wasn't a boring race," Earnhardt said following his victory, his record ninth at Atlanta.

Defending Winston Cup champion Dale Jarrett, Jimmy Spencer and other drivers had complained over the weekend of the media's reporting about the lack of lead changes and side-by-side competition in the season's first three races.

Earnhardt came to Victory Lane Sunday as if in answer to NASCAR's prayers.

"I was racing for all I could get and for all it would do," he said. "I was just driving the car as hard as I could go and giving it everything I had. It was just that time of day. It wasn't time to take it easy.

"I held (Labonte) off. It sort of seemed he was waiting, biding his time. Sure enough, he made his run there on the last lap and got close to beating us."

"I was racing for all I could get and for all it would do."

"Earnhardt Jr. climbed from the car, stood on its roof and pumped his arms skyward as confetti cannons fired all around him. He then jumped down and into his father's arms."

Dale Jr. says it all on victory lap

by David Poole

FORT WORTH, Tex.—Dale Earnhardt Jr. was out of breath and nearly speechless in victory lane Sunday after scoring his first career Winston Cup victory in the DirecTV 500 at Texas Motor Speedway.

Moments earlier, though, he had said it all.

Seconds after taking the checkered flag nearly six seconds in front of Jeff Burton's Ford, Earnhardt Jr. let his emotions go as he rolled his No. 8 Chevrolet into Turn 1 to begin his victory lap.

"Woooooooooooooooooo!" he screamed over the radio, joining his crew in celebration of a victory in the 25-year-old Winston Cup rookie's 12th career start in NASCAR's top series.

It took Tony Stewart 25 starts to get his first victory during his phenomenal rookie season a year ago. It took Davey Allison 14 starts to get a victory.

"You never really do know if you're going to win, ever. This here is awesome, man, just incredible."

—Dale Earnhardt Jr.

And it took the man who was there to meet his son in victory lane, Dale Earnhardt, 16 races to win his first Winston Cup race in 1979.

"You never really do know if you're going to win, ever," Earnhardt Jr. said after being pushed to victory lane because the clutch was gone in his race car. "Guys race and race and race for years and years and years and don't win races.

"This here is awesome, man, just incredible."

When Earnhardt reached the postrace celebration, his father and the owner of his race team stuck his head into the window.

"He just told me he loved me and he wanted to make sure I took the time to enjoy this," Earnhardt Jr. said. "You can get so swept up with what's going on around you that you don't really enjoy it yourself personally, so he just wanted me to take a minute and do this and celebrate how I wanted to celebrate."

Earnhardt Jr. climbed from the car, stood on its roof and pumped his arms skyward as confetti cannons fired all around him. He then jumped down and into his father's arms.

"He just told me he loved me and he wanted to make sure I took the time to enjoy this. You can get so swept up with what's going on around you that you don't really enjoy it yourself personally."

—Dale Earnhardt Jr.

"I'll tell you, he's something else. We knew the kid could do it. The boy drove a good race."

The Earnhardt name, of course, is a tall order to live up to. Dale Earhardt has 75 career victories, including one this year that makes him and his son the first father-son tandem to win in the same season since Bobby and Davey Allison in 1988. The elder Earnhardt, who continued his strong start to the 2000 season with a seventh-place finish Sunday, also has of course won seven Winston Cup titles and more than $37 million in his brilliant career.

Sunday's winner has a long way to go to match that kind of record. But the victory, which paid first-prize money of $374,675, was a first step just like the one the father took with his first career victory on April 1, 1979, at Bristol.

"I'll tell you, he's something else," Earnhardt said of his son. "We knew the kid could do it. The boy drove a good race."

"You're at Talladega, thinking you've got a shot to win the race, and he's just the master."

—Kenny Wallace

Earnhardt charges from 18th to front, wins

by David Poole

TALLADEGA, Ala.—Nobody can do what Dale Earnhardt did to win the Winston 500 at Talladega Superspeedway. Not even Earnhardt.

Forget what you saw. Forget what the official results show.

Nobody can be 18th with five laps to go and then have to spend the final lap worrying about being passed to have a win taken away. Nobody can run up the middle of a three-wide pack of screaming race cars and draft his way from oblivion to Victory Lane.

Nobody can do that. Not even Earnhardt.

And yet, it happened.

Earnhardt added a chapter to his legend on Sunday, roaring through traffic over the final laps in incredible fashion to win for the second time this season, the third time in four races at Talladega and the 10th time in his career at the 2.66-mile speedway.

Forget what you saw.

Forget what the official

results show.

Even Earnhardt had trouble conceiving it.

"To think anybody could come from as far back in the field as we were and win this race is beyond me," he said. "You saw it. I couldn't believe it."

How can you describe what you can't believe?

Well, for starters, the day's third caution flag came out on Lap 168 and brought the lead-pack cars in for final pit stops. Jeff Gordon had been on pit road when the yellow came after Mark Martin and Bobby Hamilton made contact behind him as they started in, too. Gordon got his tank of gas before the rest of the leaders and was up front when the green flew with 15 laps to go.

Earnhardt, meanwhile, took fuel and two tires and was 15th on the restart. He tried to start back toward the front using an outside line, but within two laps that move had punted him to 23rd. He had only improved five spots after 183 laps in the 188-lap event.

And then along came Kenny Wallace, who had four new tires on his Chevrolet and was looking for a drafting partner. When Earnhardt pulled down in front of Wallace, Joe Nemechek, Wallace's teammate on Andy Petree's team, lined up behind him, then things started happening.

"It was like I had turbos," Wallace said.

Those turbos were also pushing Earnhardt toward the front.

"I finally got on the outside of the inside line and kept working," Earnhardt said. "Kenny got in there with me along with Nemechek, and we just kept working and they pushed me to the front."

"To think anybody could come from as far back in the field as we were and win this race is beyond me. You saw it. I couldn't believe it."

Earnhardt went from 16th to eighth on Lap 185. Coming off Turn 4 on the next lap, his car popped out in front of the middle lane and he suddenly was in fourth, behind only Dale Earnhardt Jr., John Andretti and Mike Skinner.

Andretti led Lap 185. Skinner led 186. But Earnhardt was coming, and with the push from Wallace and Nemechek he was open for business. Earnhardt passed Skinner, his teammate at Richard Childress Racing, on the way to the white flag.

Earnhardt, Wallace and Nemechek were moving so fast that they pushed ahead of the pack, which bunched up racing three-wide behind them. Now, it was a matter of whether Earnhardt could hold the lead he had so miraculously attained.

"I knew they didn't want to sit behind me and run," Earnhardt said.

The fact that the front three broke clear of the rest of the traffic, however, worked against any kind of a last-lap pass by Wallace that would have been a 50th lead change and given the spine-tingling race its 22nd different leader.

"Joe and I knew what we had to do," Wallace said. "But when the three of us broke away there on the last lap, it was over because we didn't have any help."

Earnhardt did his part, of course, weaving his car down the backstretch on the final lap to break the draft and keep the teammates behind him from getting a run off the final corner. The front three raced single-file to the checkered flag, with Wallace matching his career-best finish with a second and Nemechek third after starting from the pole.

"I personally won the race for him," Wallace said of Earnhardt. "And he owes me. You're at Talladega, thinking you've got a shot to win the race, and he's just the master."

Behind the front three came Gordon, Terry Labonte and Skinner as Chevrolet swept the top six spots. As the rest of the lead pack crossed the finish line four- and even five-wide, several cars began to spin and some crashed into the wall at the end of the front-stretch. It was the only major altercation in a race that drivers had feared would be a crash-fest because of new aerodynamic rules and Saturday's last-minute NASCAR decision to reduce the size of the restrictor-plate openings from one inch to fifteen-sixteenths of an inch.

The new rules certainly had the desired effect. The 49 lead changes told only part of the story. Cars swapped positions in the running order the way 13-year-olds swap sweethearts all day long.

Nemechek started from the pole. At the end of Lap 1, he was 16th.

Gordon, who damaged his Chevrolet in Saturday's final practice and had to start from the back of the field in his backup car, had the lead on Lap 13.

With five laps remaining in the race, Earnhardt Jr. was in the lead. When the race ended he was third—third, that is, among rookies in the field. Overall, he was 14th.

"It's the wildest race I've been in in a long time. We were running four inches apart going around the corner three-wide all the way down to the bottom of the race track."

—Joe Nemechek

Winston Cup points leader Bobby Labonte was second after Lap 184. He finished 12th and lost 48 points to Earnhardt, who moved back into second in the standings ahead of Jeff Burton. Labonte's lead is now 210 points with four races remaining.

"It's the wildest race I've been in in a long time," Nemechek said. "We were running four inches apart going around the corner three-wide all the way down to the bottom of the race track."

That was before everybody really started racing after the final yellow. The final 15 laps looked like rush hour on a four-lane highway, except that the traffic jam was moving at 190 mph. In spite of that and in spite of the wreck after the checkered flag, there was a general sense that things went about as well as could be expected.

"I've got to hand it to the race drivers," Earnhardt said. "They all worked good together. It was a pretty good day, seeing that kind of racing side-by-side and three- and four-wide and nobody got in trouble. It was good, hard racing, but I still don't like restrictor-plate racing. I'm not that good at it."

He's right. Nobody's that good at it, not good enough to do what Earnhardt did.

And yet, it happened.

"I've got to hand it to the race drivers. They all worked good together. It was a pretty good day, seeing that kind of racing side-by-side and three- and four-wide and nobody got in trouble."

"This is undoubtedly one of the most difficult announcements I've ever had to make. But after the accident in Turn 4 at the end of the Daytona 500, we've lost Dale Earnhardt."

—NASCAR president Mike Helton

You knew it was bad

by Ron Green

DAYTONA BEACH, Fla.—He had moved through his career like smoke, his race car rushing toward openings, some visible only to him, openings through which he drove to seven Winston Cup championships and a place in racing history.

He had seemed invincible, escaping the wrecks around him, recovering control as no one else could when his car began to do a deadly dance out there on the asphalt, quieting it the way you might quiet a skittish colt.

When there was a thump, a bump, a fender to be thrust out to claim a foot or two of the race track, he was the one nobody wanted to tangle with, the one nobody wanted owing them "a lick," as they say in racing. He was The Intimidator. He drove like the son of a moonshiner, like the spirit of stock car racing in its primitive form, with a roar and a wicked smile and an artistic bumper.

Sunday, in the late afternoon sunshine at the Daytona International Speedway, it all turned around.

On the last lap of the Daytona 500, somebody shouldered him, and this time Dale Earnhardt couldn't rein in his black Chevrolet with the number 3, the most recognizable number in auto racing, on its side. His car turned sideways, slid up the track and crashed head-on into the concrete wall, and you knew it was bad.

Darrell Waltrip, in a moment of raw human emotion for sports television, was doing commentary and was weeping with joy over his brother Michael's victory in the Daytona 500, Michael's first victory ever after 400-some starts. But Darrell's happiness was soon muted by the wreckage that he saw down there in the grass. Workmen and medics were taking a long time to get Earnhardt out of his battered car.

Those are the bad ones, Darrell had told us, the ones where you run headfirst into the wall.

Those, he said, are the ones that hurt you.

We waited, feeling the warmth of Michael Waltrip's victory, but at the same time feeling the chill of hurt, maybe worse. The concern only worsened when TV showed Dale Earnhardt Jr., who had just finished second in perhaps the finest performance of his young career, running to his dad, and then showed the ambulance carrying Earnhardt Sr. driving down that asphalt where he has won so many races and where on this day he had distinguished himself not only

Sunday, in the late afternoon sunshine at the Daytona International Speedway, it all turned around.

He's hurt, we thought, but he'll be OK. He's Dale Earnhardt. He's the greatest there ever was.

as a driver but as a father and a car owner as well. They were taking him to a nearby hospital. Someone asked Ken Schrader, who had run into Earnhardt's sliding car and who had climbed out of his wreck to check on Earnhardt, what Earnhardt's condition was. Schrader, his face a mask of concern, said he wasn't a doctor and didn't want to speculate. That sounded bad.

He's hurt, we thought, but he'll be OK. He's Dale Earnhardt. He's the greatest there ever was.

He's the one whose fans needed only to put his number—3— on their car windows to let us know where their loyalties lay. But he wasn't OK. Dale Earnhardt, the best there ever was, the face and the heart and the soul of stock car racing, died of his injuries. We heard this and we thought, no, Dale Earnhardt doesn't die, not after all the danger he's lived through, not after all the artistic driving he has done when trouble was chasing him, not after he had winked at us and smiled that crooked smile beneath that bushy mustache and made us think another championship was coming, and if it didn't, somebody was going to have to drive the wheels off a car to stop it.

If "Three" had to go on a race track though, he could not have found a more appropriate time, if there is such a thing. He was at Daytona, driving in The Great American Race. And he died on the day when he had seemed the most human he had ever seemed on a race track.

And you can believe this—if he could, Dale Earnhardt wouldn't fuss about the accident. He would say, "That's racin'."

On this day, he was like a mother hen. He had hired Michael Waltrip to drive one of his team cars and people had asked why, because Michael Waltrip had never won a regular Winston Cup race.

And he had given his son, Dale Jr., the team's other ride. Now, with the laps winding down at Daytona, there was Waltrip in first, Dale Jr. in second and Daddy in third. Daddy kept his bumper wide, holding off any and all who tried to overtake his boys.

He got his boys safely home, Waltrip winning, Dale Jr. riding shotgun, but on that awful last lap, he drifted back and into traffic, and somebody's fender tagged him and sent him on his way to screeching, smoking, thunderous death. And you can believe this— if he could, Dale Earnhardt wouldn't fuss about the accident. He would say, "That's racin'."

Stock car racing is rapidly becoming huge on the American sports scene. Nobody has had more to do with that than "Three." Dale Earnhardt was the embodiment of stock car racing. He was its most honest image. He was dark speed, an Elvis smile, a blithe spirit who knew that racing was just that, racing, and really all the rules you needed were to race like a man and keep the pedal on the floor.

Now, if you'll pardon me, I'm going to go cry.

He was dark speed, an Elvis smile, a blithe spirit who knew that racing was just that, racing. . . .

"The thoughts about Earnhardt will linger, of course. The memories will last long after the flowers wither. And at some point the funny stories will be funny again, and the sad ones won't hurt quite as much, and all that is the way it should be."

Quiet salute to the man who took us by a roar

by Tommy Tomlinson

CHARLOTTE, N.C.—The fans walked up, but they did not speak. The police lights flashed, but there were no sirens. The cars came by the hundreds, but all you heard was wet tires on pavement, shhhhh.

Early in the morning it snowed to the north and rained to the south. But then the clouds backed away. Dale Earnhardt's family has asked for as private a moment as the world could give. Even the weather obliged.

Only a few dozen fans showed up outside Calvary Church. The sanctuary holds thousands of people, but to get into Earnhardt's memorial service, you had to have an invitation. No one outside made a fuss. They went off for a smoke under the sweetgum trees, or talked to the reporters, or just stood there on the lawn, watching the door.

Everybody else stayed away.

Some NASCAR fans cross the country during racing season, showing up at the track a week early, cheering practice laps, buying scanners so they can listen to a driver talk

to his pit crew. Since Earnhardt died at Daytona on Sunday, thousands of them have left flowers and candles and poems at Earnhardt's shop in Mooresville. Thousands more have called radio stations and signed books at funeral homes.

But on Thursday they honored Earnhardt by staying out of the way of his family and friends.

Just before 11 a.m., two police cars came around the curve on Rea Road just south of the church. Behind the cars were six black limousines, and behind the limousines were 11 buses, and in the window of each bus was a piece of paper with Earnhardt's No. 3.

A fan on the sidewalk took off his 3 hat as the caravan passed. The South County Regional Library, across the street from the church, had a 3 painted in the window. A truck at the top of the hill had a 3 etched in the dirt on its back doors.

Our world seems to get louder every day, more crude and more dismissive of other people's feelings, so it almost seems strange when a big event is quiet and subtle. The Earnhardt family held a small private funeral on Wednesday, and some fans surely wished for more than Thursday's simple service. But there is power in understatement. It leaves room for people to sort out their thoughts.

The thoughts about Earnhardt will linger, of course. The memories will last long after the flowers wither. And at some point the funny stories will be funny again, and the sad ones won't hurt quite as much, and all that is the way it should be.

People need flowers and funerals, symbols and rituals, in the same way a song needs a chorus. No matter how far we travel, or how fast, we need something to bring us back home, and push us back out again.

The service ended a little early, but even so, many of the fans outside the church had already left. The mourners loaded into the cars and limousines and buses. The line crawled out of the parking lot. All these people whose lives revolve around fast cars, and now the wheels turned so slow.

But around the corner, not far off, they would come up on a highway.

Requests pour in for songs Owen performed in tribute

They were close enough friends to have stayed at each other's homes, so it was only natural that Alabama lead singer Randy Owen would choose one of his own songs to sing at Dale Earnhardt's memorial service.

That song, "Goodbye (Kelly's Song)" is a little-known cut from the group's 1990 album "Pass I t on Down." Though the lyrics fit the memorial perfectly, it has actually been written as an apology to his wife, Kelly, for all the times he left to tour with his band.

"Goodbye, goodbye, till I see you again. Goodbye, goodbye, I'll love and I'll miss you till then. That one word hurts so bad, You lose a friend you've had. But you keep the faith and pray to return."

Owen wouldn't comment on his participation in the memorial or why he sang that particular song. But almost as soon as the service ended, the band's record label, RCA, began receiving calls from around the country, and radio stations began airing it.

Also getting a lot of play was the other song Owen chose to sing, the better-known Alabama hit "Angels Among Us." Originally released in 1993, that song has become a sort of anthem for people who have suffered greatly or died young, with lyrics about angels in our darkest hours.

"Goodbye, goodbye, till I see you again."

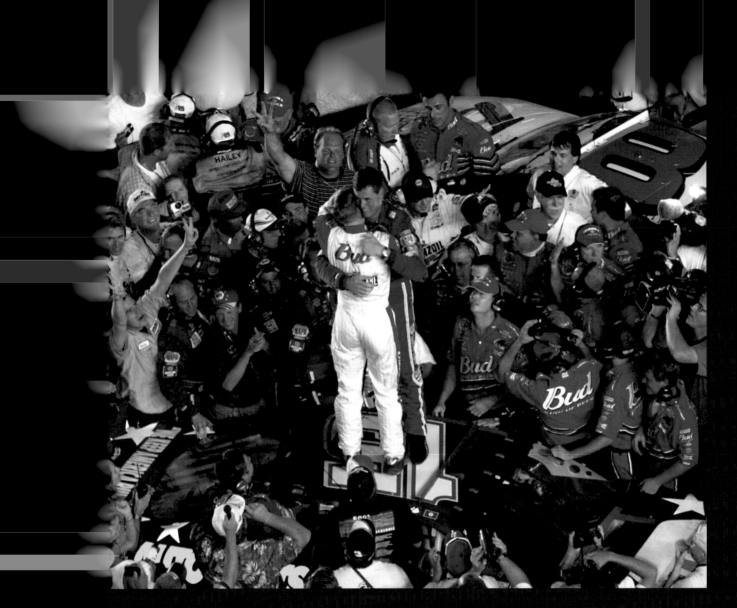

"He was with me tonight. I don't know how I did it. I dedicate this win to him. I want to say hey to Teresa back home. I hope she's loving this, because we sure are."

—Dale Earnhardt Jr.

Dale Jr. conjures up stirring victory in Pepsi 400

by David Poole

DAYTONA BEACH, Fla.—In a style reminiscent of his father and the man whose memory still dominates this place and this sport, Dale Earnhardt Jr. scored an emotional victory in the Pepsi 400 at Daytona International Speedway Saturday night.

Earnhardt Jr. had dominated the race in his No. 8 Chevrolet, but was forced to come from seventh to first in the final six laps after a crash during the final round of pit stops threatened to cost him the victory.

It took him less than two, and it was a spine-tingling moment when he swept past Johnny Benson in Turn 4 on Lap 156—very near the spot where his father, seven-time Winston Cup champion Dale Earnhardt, crashed on the final lap of the Daytona 500 and died on Feb. 18.

Teammate Michael Waltrip, first with Earnhardt Jr. second in that ill-fated season opener, worked his way up to second this time and stayed right there, where Earnhardt Jr. had stayed in February. Elliott Sadler followed Waltrip through traffic over the final laps, but on this night Earnhardt Jr. was not to be denied.

"Man, I just don't know what to say," Earnhardt Jr. said after spinning his car in celebration in the same spot on the infield grass where his father had done so following his Daytona 500 victory in 1998.

"He was with me tonight," Earnhardt Jr. said of Earnhardt. " I don't know how I did it. I dedicate this win to him. I want to say hey to Teresa (Earnhardt's widow) back home. I hope she's loving this, because we sure are."

Earnhardt Jr. had climbed to the window of his car and saluted the cheering crowd. Waltrip pulled his Chevrolet alongside the winner's and joined the celebration as their teams ran to meet them. The drivers hugged on top of Waltrip's No. 15 Chevrolet before Earnhardt dove headlong into the arms of his waiting crew.

After they finally made it to victory lane, Earnhardt's crew ran back across the grass and the frontstretch to greet the fans during a post-race fireworks display that doubled as a tribute to Earnhardt's memory.

It was a remarkable scene, and a remarkable scenario that was set into motion on Lap 142, as the leaders were thinking about when to come in for their final pit stops.

"Man, I just don't know what to say." —Dale Earnhardt Jr.

As Mike Wallace tried to go to pit lane, Mike Skinner slowed slightly to avoid him and got hit from behind by Kurt Busch. Skinner slammed the wall and cars started wrecking. Ten cars were damaged in all and several others had to take evasive action.

Earnhardt Jr. was ahead of the wreck and hadn't pitted, so he came in on Lap 145 under yellow with the rest of the leaders. He took four tires—many of those who'd stopped before the yellow had taken only two—and got off pit road first among those who pitted under yellow.

Six other cars, however, were ahead of him on the restart. All—Benson, Dave Blaney, Ken Schrader, Jeremy Mayfield, Tony Stewart and Bobby Labonte—had pitted under green just before the yellow.

The green flew on Lap 150 with 11 laps left. In Turn 4 on the first lap back under green, however, the Chevrolet driven by points leader Jeff Gordon started smoking badly. Gordon had been damaged in the Lap 142 wreck, and his problems brought out another yellow.

That was a break for Earnhardt Jr., since the single-file restart with six laps to go meant no lapped cars would be underneath him as he tried to fight his way back to the lead.

He was fourth by Turn 4 and third at the line on the first lap after green. He swept past Blaney into second on the backstretch of Lap 156, then passed Benson in Turn 4 and had the lead. Once he was there, he wasn't about to give it up, and Waltrip's ability to get right behind him provided a nice bit of insurance.

"When I got there, there were two to go," Waltrip said. "Quite frankly, I was thankful. At the end of the race, I just pushed him. I am just so thankful that he won, first of all, and that I was able to fight my way up through there and run second so I could be part of his celebration."

"I am just so thankful that he won, first of all, and that I was able to fight my way up through there and run second so I could be part of his celebration."

—Michael Waltrip

Credits

GarPro Communications, Lexington, NC: Narration written and recorded by Mark Garrow; audio research and production by Steve Richards.

Concentrix Music and Sound Design, Charlotte, NC: All music, recording, editing, mixing and CD premastering by Concentrix; engineered and mixed by Michael McGinnis and Anthony Fedele; production assistance by Fred Story and Melissa Curlin.

Archival audio provided by and copyright of **GarPro Communications; Performance Racing Network/SMI;** and **MRN Radio,** a division of **International Speedway Corporation.**

FRONT COVER PHOTOS:
Top row, left to right—Jeff Siner, The Charlotte Observer; Davie Hinshaw, The Charlotte Observer; Christopher A. Record, The Charlotte Observer; Bottom row, left to right—Mark B. Sluder, The Charlotte Observer; Jeff Siner, The Charlotte Observer; Paul Kizzle, AP/Wide World Photos.

BACK COVER PHOTO:
Chris O'Meara, AP/Wide World Photos

INTERIOR PHOTOS:
The Charlotte Observer
Bill Billings—9, 14, 15, 24
David T. Foster III—105 (bottom)
Tom Franklin—18
Milton Hinnant—28
Davie Hinshaw—19, 35, 43, 61, 94, 157
Don Hunter—8, 10, 13, 17, 20, 36, 37
Francisco Kjolseth—115, 150 (bottom)
Diedra Laird—40, 56, 72
Bob Leverone—98
Gary O'Brien—49, 68
Christopher A. Record—60, 83, 86, 90, 95, 99, 105 (top), 120, 124, 150 (top),155 (top)

Patrick Schneider—42, 121, 127, 138, 154 (top), 158, 159
Jeff Siner—1, 44, 53, 81, 102, 106, 110, 111, 112, 113 (top and bottom), 114, 116, 119, 123, 128, 130, 133, 139 (top), 147, 149 (top and bottom), 152, 153, 155 (bottom)
Mark B. Sluder—21, 46, 48, 51, 55, 64, 73, 76, 82 (top and bottom), 84, 89, 92, 103, 107
Todd Sumlin—122, 154 (bottom)
Dick Van Halseman—50
Fred Wilson—29, 30, 32, 33

AP/Wide World Photos
Bruce Ackerman—97, 148 (top)
Dale Atkins—125
Ed Bailey—93
Bob Brodbeck—39
Rusty Burroughs—109
Chuck Burton—26, 78
Mary Ann Chastain—131
Phil Coale—143
Jim Cole—63
David Duprey—67
Ric Feld—71, 132, 134
Mark Foley—23 (left), 38, 45

Darryl Graham—75
Bill Grimshaw—139 (bottom)
Tony Gutierrez—146
Mark Humphrey—59
Paul Kizzle—151 (bottom)
Jay LaPrete—140
Chuck Luzier—6
Alan Marler—145
Dave Martin—31
Donna McWilliam—126, 136
Chuck McQuinn—151 (top)
Chris O'Meara—74, 79, 87, 117, 135
Terry Renna—80
Reed Saxon—12, 16
Jay Sailors—54
Bill Sikes—100
Steve Simoneau—156
Glen Smith—151 (middle)
Tom Strattman—88
Bob Sweeten—101
Toby Talbot—27
Christine Wetzel—22
Russell Williams—5
Larry Woodall—23 (right), 34

We would like to thank the many people at The Charlotte Observer who have worked tirelessly over the past three decades to bring the story of Dale Earnhardt's incredible racing career to the pages of the paper every day. Special thanks for their support on this project go to Peter Vandevanter, Davie Hinshaw, Mike Persinger, Gary Schwab, Kathy Persinger, John Simmons, David Poole and Joan Baker.

MARK GARROW serves as co-anchor for the race broadcasts on The Performance Racing Network (PRN). He also hosts PRN's Garage Pass, a daily show heard on over 450 radio stations nationwide and NASCAR.com, providing fans with the latest NASCAR news and an insider's look at what's really going on "behind the fence." Considered one of the hardest working broadcasters in motorsports today, Mark has earned numerous awards for his work over the last 19 years. Mark resides near Lexington, NC, with his wife, Lynne, and their children, Breanna and Marissa.